JANAKI LENIN writes about a quarter century of adventures with animals while living with snakeman Rom Whitaker. She examines the behaviour of humans with the same droll perspective. Janaki and Rom live on a farm with Momo, Burru, Amba, and Chola (dogs), Neelakanta (emu), and Luppy (pig).

Love,
David cousins

My Husband and Other Animals 2

The Wildlife Adventure Continues

JANAKI LENIN

Illustrated by Gynelle Alves

First published by Westland Publications Private Limited in 2018
61, 2nd Floor, Silverline Building, Alapakkam Main Road,
Maduravoyal, Chennai 600095

Westland and the Westland logo are the trademarks of Westland
Publications Private Limited, or its affiliates.

ISBN: 9789386850928

10 9 8 7 6 5 4 3 2 1

Typeset by Ram Das Lal, New Delhi, NCR
Printed at Manipal Technologies Limited, Manipal

Contents

Introduction

Janaki, who is my *Pistola*, is captivated by the creatures we share life with, from our pack of dogs to wild king cobras. She experiences them in ways I tend to miss, opening up new vistas of animal smarts and behaviour. Ever since our local leopard took centre stage, sharpening our senses, we've been pulled into deeper communion with the jackals, porcupines, civet cats, monkeys, birds, reptiles, trees, plants and insects that share our farm.

We've lived here at Pambukudivanam for 20 years now and many are the trees we planted that you can't put your arms around. Orioles, treepies, woodpeckers, kingfishers, spotted owlets and parakeets also call it home, and the resident ratsnake regularly sheds his 7-foot-long skin below the expansive banyan tree shading our house. Indian eagle owls hoot each evening from Karadi Malai, the forested hill in front of us and in the early morning sun the pair of booted eagles soar.

While others might be happy to just watch these

creatures, Janaki goes many steps further. Her fixation with animal poop for example is in another league: is that rat shit or frog shit on the kitchen counter, let's wash the leopard scat and see what he's been eating, and could that mysterious animal that left the ant-filled dump have been a pangolin?

All my life I've been a reptile nut, and for the first decade of our lives together, Janaki joined me in my pursuits as herpetologist, filmmaker, and communicator. Perhaps tiring of my single-track mind, she struck out on her own, making friends with professionals who study mammals, birds and insects. Her stories are drawn from tracking these field biologists, our own adventures, and her deep fascination with the natural world.

Janaki weaves our travels to the Agumbe rainforest, Andaman islands, Assam and other locales into a wonderful magic-carpet ride. She's also prone to disappearing down the proverbial rabbit hole in the quest for answers: why didn't the fishing cat make it down to south India (or did it?) and how the hell do oystercatchers teach their young to shuck oysters and clams? Until she finds answers, she's as restless as a mama cat with her kittens.

These stories are mostly taken from her four-year-long string for *The Hindu* and share some similarities with the earlier volume, but here she also waxes scientific. She balances animal tales with personal stories such as how we met *Falling in Love* and how we became partners *Marriages are Made on Earth* and some serious pieces like *Why do Men Rape,* and *An Appeal to Nature*, and *Why Did Homosexuality Evolve* that have deep insights into human behaviour.

In the best tradition of the Indian snack called *mixture*, this collection has equal parts of the whimsical, serious, tragic, and hilarious.

Romulus Whitaker
Pambukudivanam
20 October 2017

Hype of the Tiger

When the first volume of *My Husband and Other Animals* was published, I asked a friend for marketing advice. Her first question was, 'Have you written about tigers?'

'No, I haven't.'

Although the friend moved on to other questions, I imagine others will ask me the same thing.

A shiver of excitement runs through friends when they describe their encounters with tigers. For many, the sight of a large cat striding regally down a forest path is what sparks their lifelong interest in wildlife. My interest in animals was, however, ignited in the backyard of my parents' home in the city.

When I met Rom, he showed me cobras in neighbouring rice fields, monitor lizards in rock piles, and chameleons on trees near pump houses. During the monsoon, we visited seasonal ponds in casuarina plantations along the coast near the Madras Crocodile Bank to see frogs and toads. If the season was right, we spent hours on the beach watching the waves glow with the eerie blue-green luminescence of plankton. 'What is nature; what is the wild' confuse me. On winter nights, trees flashed with the courtship displays of thousands of fireflies. After experiences such as these, questions such as 'What is nature; where is the wild?' confuse me.

Rom took me to forests, too, but to the wettest ones where rare snakes, lizards, and frogs live. The chances of seeing a tiger there were very low. We also spent a lot of time in the Andaman Islands where there are no tigers. We were not interested in the forests of central India for a simple reason: they may be great for tigers, but not for the creatures we sought.

I finally 'saw' my first tiger in Bandipur, in 2005, on a family holiday. We didn't see enough of it to say we saw a tiger, but neither could we say we saw nothing. The news reached the hotel ahead of us, and everyone greeted us as if we had seen Brad Pitt and Salman Khan, hand-in-hand. I don't remember anyone expressing as much excitement when Rom and I watched the glorious spectacle of a pair of big male king cobras wrestling for a full two hours.

A few years after the visit to Bandipur, we travelled to Bandhavgarh. Rom was to present a short movie showcasing India's chief wildlife tourism asset—the tiger. When someone spotted the striped cat, word went out, and safari jeeps raced down dirt roads, eager to get their clients there before the animal moved. Not unlike how poachers operate, I imagine.

The forest department conducted 'tiger shows'. Tame elephants cornered a tiger in an inaccessible spot, and for a price, tourists were taken on elephant-back to see the obviously bored cat. It wasn't a wildlife park so much as an open-air zoo experience. Unlike many of the other creatures for whom we waited hours and hours and made numerous journeys into the forest before being blessed with a sight, here tigers materialized as instantly as they do on television. It didn't have the quality of a wildlife documentary as much as a wildlife *Big Brother*.

Outside the park, we saw sarus cranes fling their heads up in the air and call raucously as they danced in fallow wheat fields. The birds seemed freer than those poor tigers imprisoned in 'the wild'.

I don't deny the tiger is a magnificent animal, but it has also become a commodity—for hunters, conservationists, poachers, tourists, entrepreneurs, photographers, researchers, rheumatic Chinese, and for countless writers—for a long time.

When you read the adventures of big-game hunters in Africa or Asia, there is invariably a 'menacing' mamba or an 'aggressive' cobra they dispatch to prove their machismo. In my writing career, I naturally correct this imbalance by giving snakes and other less charismatic animals their rightful place in the galaxy of wildlife stars. Now you see why I don't write about tigers. I hope readers will forgive my bloody-mindedness!

The American Mongoose

I caught the masked ransacker red-handed. He had opened my bag and thrown my clothes and things around. Seated comfortably, cushioned amongst my clothes, he was engrossed in 'washing' something, by rubbing his hands together. He looked up at me as if to ask, 'Did you want something?' The raccoon had found a bag of peanuts, and flakes of the nuts' brown skin lay sprinkled over my things. I carried the creature to the living room, where his cage stood empty and set him on the carpeted floor.

We had arrived moments earlier at the home of our friends, the Clamps, in Edisto Island, South Carolina. I ought not to have been surprised by the raccoon, since Sharon was known to adopt orphaned cubs.

As I watched the raccoon waddle across the floor, Sharon told me his mum had been run over while crossing a busy highway. The cub was too young to fend for himself. His curiosity, intelligence, and fearlessness reminded me of mongooses moving in slow motion. I had never seen a live raccoon before, and this was a delightful introduction.

Sharon said almost all her raccoons were quick to take to the wild. They ate anything, and could live anywhere. This lack of fussiness has stood the animals in good stead. The time we spent with the Clamps didn't prepare me for my next raccoon experience.

A few days later, we were visiting a friend in West Virginia. It was late night when we returned to his home in the suburbs. JM slowed down to swing into the driveway and startled a raccoon that had been rummaging in the garbage bin. JM swore and cursed. The animals were disease-infested pests, he ranted.

In cities, garbage and pet food are plentiful year-round. Out in the American countryside, the animals forage for insects, fruits, nuts, and birds' eggs. It is not surprising there are more raccoons compressed into urban areas than in rural farmlands.

Urban parks, such as Hugh Taylor Birch State Park in Fort Lauderdale, Florida, and Rock Creek Park in Washington, D.C., hold dense populations of raccoons, a couple of hundred plus per square kilometre. In comparison, the countryside has between four to 400 times fewer raccoons.

As if the plentiful garbage available on every street were not enough, some people, like JM's neighbour, just can't resist feeding these animals. This drives our friend apoplectic with rage.

Unperturbed by the acrimonious neighbourly relations, one raccoon made a den in another resident's attic. Looking at that leafy suburb, I imagined raccoons enjoyed a better standard of living in cities than in the country.

However, life is not all hunky-dory for these freeloaders.

Living off garbage has its price. Biologists have found plastic, rubber bands, and other indigestible objects in raccoon scat. Instead of fearsome predators and hunters, disease and road accidents kill a good percentage of citified raccoons.

With help from humans, raccoons have even crossed the Atlantic and colonized Europe. During the Second World War, some American soldiers kept raccoons as pets. When the men's tour of duty ended, a few released their captives. In addition, a few escaped from raccoon fur farms established in eastern Europe. In a misguided attempt to 'enrich' the native fauna, some were deliberately released in a German forest during the Nazi era. Now there are breeding populations in many European countries.

In southeastern United States, raccoons wander along beaches feasting on sea turtle eggs, while in Europe, birds are especially vulnerable to their depredations. I find it hard to think of these cute creatures as pests, and I imagine the work of conservationists who have to control raccoon numbers must be tough.

If only all animals were as cute and capable of exploiting humans, we wouldn't need to worry about their conservation.

Chicken Soup for the Jungle Chicken's Soul

'Look! Jungle chicken,' I whispered. Rom cut the engine, expecting the foreign cameraman to get a shot of the gorgeous scimitar-tailed rooster rooting in a small forest opening. When I realized he was neither filming nor intended to, I whispered, 'Get a shot of it.' Before he could get his camera set up, it scurried into a bush.

'Ah, it's just a chicken,' he said.

Little did he realize just how special these birds are.

There are three jungle chickens in the subcontinent: the red, the grey, and the Sri Lankan. The red chicken occurs towards the east and north of India, the grey in the south and west, and the Sri Lankan, the prettiest of them all, belongs to the island nation. Domestic chickens are believed to be descendants of the reds with some grey thrown in.

When I began visiting the forests of the Western Ghats

with Rom, about twenty years ago, I heard the roosters' distinctive crowing at dawn, but it was difficult to see one. Instead, all I saw were swaying shrubs where the birds had been grubbing moments earlier.

On one occasion, we saw a whole flock of colourful chickens scratching in the dirt, in a forest. My excitement turned to disappointment when we came upon a hamlet. Those birds were domestic chickens with a lot of wild blood.

Free-ranging chickens were by no means plentiful enough to feed a family regularly. Battery-farmed chickens weren't available in shops at that time. So anyone who had a firearm went hunting. And the birds turned wary of all humans.

Over the years, I've been seeing more and more of these birds in our forays into the jungle. Whenever we visit the Agumbe Rainforest Research Station, we watch a flock of grey jungle fowl pecking in the open, on misty mornings. We always remark as we shake our heads in disbelief, 'Twenty years ago, we never imagined this was possible.'

What led to this remarkable change? Some biologist friends wonder whether increased protection of wildlife gave the jungle chicken a reprieve. But I'm not aware of other species making such a remarkable comeback. Or perhaps the birds have become acclimatized to human presence because more wildlife-lovers are going into the jungle. Maybe so.

'It's the price of

cartridges,' Rom says. 'It's too expensive now to waste on a small bird like a chicken. Hunters would rather go for large mammals.' But I have my own theory. The increase in jungle chicken numbers may be related to the plummeting fortunes of wild fish.

Aaron Savio Lobo, a marine biologist, looked at the economics of the trawling industry. In our oceans, trawl nets sweep for shrimp, tuna, and snappers. But the enormous nets catch everything else in their paths, too. Fishermen saved desirable fish for the market and dumped a large percentage of the catch in the sea as trash. Over the years, profit margins shrank as fish populations collapsed. The trawlers turned to yesterday's waste to stay afloat. Trash fish is now processed into chicken feed, the mainstay of a burgeoning chicken farming industry.

The more broiler chicken we saw at the market, the more grey jungle chicken we began seeing in the forests. Maybe the relationship between increasing farmed chicken sales and the higher visibility of their wild cousins is mere coincidence.

The Northeast offers a counterpoint. Battery-farmed chickens haven't made inroads, and tribal communities hunt wild animals for sustenance. Upset by the harm to wildlife and oblivious of the catastrophe occurring in our seas, many mainland conservationists say with the disdain of Marie Antoinette, 'Let them eat farmed chicken.'

When our territorial waters turn into aquatic deserts devoid of fish, what will be the fate of trawlers, the chicken industry, and jungle chickens?

At least for now, in the south, jungle chickens have it good.

Scientific Palmistry

I had not examined my right hand since my high school days, when my friends and I tried to divine each other's future. The middle finger stood tallest, followed by the ring finger, and then the index. In my other hand, I held a science magazine with an illustration of a 'masculine' hand. It looked like mine. Apparently, the index finger on a typical 'feminine' hand is almost the same length as the ring finger.

The magazine went on to say what the implication of the long ring finger was: I had received more testosterone in my mother's womb. Estrogen would have made my index finger longer. Finger lengths are obvious indicators of hormonal activity at a crucial time in foetal development.

Hundreds of studies link finger length ratio to pretty much

everything: behaviour, cognition, personality traits, length and size of body parts, diseases, and more. One study said people with my kind of hand are more likely to show mental toughness, optimism and aggression. But my 'masculine' hand also predisposed me towards drug or alcohol addiction, left-handedness, athleticism, and disinterest in babies. My chances of landing in prison, going mad, or being murdered were high.

Another study suggested that people with male hands were less adept at gauging the moods of people in photographs. As a film editor, I had cut between shots of actors' faces to elicit drama, comedy, and pathos in innumerable scenes and episodes of television series. Had I done this without being able to read faces? Give me a break!

I researched where a feminine hand would take me: high risk of breast cancer, schizophrenia, eczema, and hay fever. A longer index finger also indicated the person had better verbal and literary skills. Did I blow my chance of being a good writer while still in my mother's womb?

For some inexplicable reason, prenatal sex hormones only affected the finger lengths of the right hand. I measured the two offending fingers and divided the length of the index by the length of the ring finger. The ratio was 0.95, an average male hand. Women with feminine hands should have a ratio close to one since their index and ring fingers are of equal length.

It even works in animals. Rats injected with testosterone produce babies with longer fourth digits in their right foot. This digit corresponds to ring fingers in our hands. High-ranking female rhesus macaques had longer ring fingers than lower ranking ones, said one study.

Then came the surprise: long ring fingers make us a successful species. Besides using fire, humans are unique in their ability to throw spears and use slingshots. Long ring fingers stabilize the middle finger, providing greater accuracy in hitting the target, said one study. It's possible that men with long ring fingers, who brought home the bacon more frequently, were preferred mates.

Our destiny is in our hands. But I remain unconvinced. Some studies drew conclusions from examining a few people. Many results were contested by others. The methodology was inconsistent: some measured left hands, while one got impossible ratios. Some traits like finger length could be inherited. Reading these studies was more entertaining than enlightening, like reading on personality types according to zodiac signs.

My eyes were bleary from reading too long when Rom enquired about my progress. 'The finger ratio can tell two things—prenatal exposure to sex hormones, and, maybe, sexual orientation,' I replied.

Rom asked, 'And?'

'And what?'

'What's your sexual orientation?'

'Possibly lesbianism,' my voice dropped a notch.

With a broad grin and a suggestive look, he commented, 'That could be interesting.'

He held up his own right hand. In the 1960s, he had been bitten by a prairie rattler, and his index finger was obviously stunted.

'In my case, it shows my stupidity,' he said ruefully.

Break a Finger

When Rom woke up from Demerol-induced sleep, he asked the pretty woman in white bending over him, 'Am I in heaven?'

He had been bitten by a prairie rattlesnake while snake-hunting in the Chihuahua desert near El Paso, Texas, in 1966. His arm swelled rapidly, and he knew he was in trouble. At the emergency room in the William Beaumont Hospital, where he was stationed as a conscript of the US army, Rom expected to be treated with antivenom. But medics also wrapped a pressure cuff on his arm. He knew enough about snakebite treatment to know that was not recommended procedure. What followed was worse.

Rom's severely swollen arm was placed in a container of ice, and doctors gave him Demerol for the excruciating pain. Dr Herbert Stahnke of Arizona State University advocated the use of cryotherapy in snakebite treatment. He believed the combination of pressure cuff and ice would retard the spread of venom into the body, while slowing tissue destruction. Rom was one of several snakebite victims of that time to undergo this experimental treatment.

Even in his Demerol-haze, he suspected cryotherapy was going to complicate his recovery, but the army doctors were deaf to his protests.

Three days later, the medics allowed his arm to thaw and the pain worsened. Eventually, the swelling subsided, the open wound caused by the venom healed, and he was discharged. But he lost the use of his trigger finger.

In 1971, Dr Hugh Frank reviewed cryotherapy in snakebite treatment and concluded it caused more tissue damage than snake venom. While later victims were spared the torture of having their limb frozen and thawed, could Rom's finger have been saved had the doctors listened to him? It's hard to say for certain. The agonizing treatment taught him to be extra careful when handling venomous snakes, and he didn't suffer another serious snakebite again.

Rom survived in better shape than several of his snake-hunting colleagues. Shaking their hands is like shaking lobsters' claws; many of their fingers are missing, deformed, or partly amputated.

Rom's saga with the mistreated snakebite didn't end for five years. Synovial fluid, the joint lubricant, leaked copiously from the nail cuticle. Doctors tried various treatments and failed. He grew used to changing bandages every day, but he never became accustomed to the smell.

After Rom moved to Madras in 1969, he sought the help of Irula medicine man, Chokalingam. He made a paste from the root of a particular plant and applied it on the finger every day. Two weeks later, it healed completely but remained calcified, numb and useless. Dr Findlay Russell, a well-known authority on snakebites, advised him to amputate it if it bothered him.

Annamalai, one of our Irula snake-hunting buddies, had a withered, bony finger from a cobra bite. It got in his way, and one day, out of exasperation, he broke it off and threw it into the bushes. Rom's young sons and nephew thought that was cool. They urged Rom to break off his finger as well.

In its place, one son suggested he could fix a snake hook, like the iron hook-arm of Captain James Hook, the fictional pirate enemy of Peter Pan. The other son felt it had to be a collapsible fishing rod. The nephew thought a multi-tool Swiss Army knife would be handier. What about a snake tongs attachment? Should it be part of a customized snake hunters' Swiss Army knife? The Whitaker line of prosthetic finger accessories sounded better than the finger itself.

Much to the disappointment of the boys, Rom wasn't swayed by their enthusiastic ideas. Then the movie *Edward Scissorhands* came out, and a raging debate broke out once more.

'Old snake hunters never die; they just rot away,' Rom said while shaking his bum finger.

Single-minded to a Fault

We were sipping tea in Maria's living room when Amit, her five-year-old son, walked in. Circular clumps of thick muck adhered to the kid's knees, and he was carrying more dirt in his tightly clenched hands. A trail of muddy footprints marked his progress across the immaculate room. Oblivious to his mother's distress at his appearance, Amit made straight for Rom to show him a precious frog he had unearthed in the garden. After Rom had made appreciative noises, Maria shooed him out of the house, telling him to go clean up, pronto.

'When did you first start catching snakes, Rom?' she asked.

'Oh, when I was four years old,' Rom replied.

I guess she had expected Rom to say he had been an adult. She had been complaining that Amit was always mucking about in the dirt and bringing frogs home. She hoped he would grow out of his obsession with the slimy creatures. But Rom's reply hung a question mark over that hope.

Rom had been interested in snakes from the time he turned a log over in his aunt's garden in upstate New York and found a harmless milk snake. Since then, he knew he wanted  to spend his life working with the creatures. As a young adult, he did assorted temporary jobs to survive.

When you live with someone who has a singularity of purpose, you wonder about your own lack of one. When I was growing up, almost every adult I met asked me the same question, 'What are you going to be when you grow up?' I answered with whatever came to mind: doctor, teacher, airplane pilot. If my answer met approval, I repeated it a few more times. I once answered 'housewife' and immediately drew sharp disapproval. I didn't ask why so many women in the family chose an inappropriate career.

After school, I decided to become a film editor. I wasn't driven by a life-defining interest. Even while studying to be an editor, I was learning Sanskrit, Carnatic music, and karate. Then when I said I wanted to learn tai-chi, my father lost patience. He said I was interested in too many things and lacked focus.

When you don't have a single overriding interest, any obstacle becomes larger than the goal. During the latter part of my fifteen-year career in television, I struggled to keep my eyes on the target. That's part of the reason I admire filmmakers like Satyajit Ray. Despite many obstacles, sometimes lasting years, he never lost sight of the film. I wasn't made of such stern stuff.

Then I switched careers and worried, 'Will I be able to earn a living?'

'Just focus on writing,' Rom replied. 'Don't worry about the money. It will all fall into place.'

'How?' I demanded.

'If someone had asked me fifty years ago, how I would earn a living working with snakes, I wouldn't have been able to answer. But I didn't do badly, did I?'

You could say I'm like Yudhistira, the eldest of the Pandava brothers, in the Indian epic Mahabharata. Drona, their teacher, set out a wooden bird as a target. He asked each brother in turn, 'What do you see?'

'I see trees, my brothers, and the bird,' Yudhistra replied.

'I see the eye of the bird,' replied Arjuna. Rom is like Arjuna.

Sometime after that conversation at Maria's home, Amit's parents took him to a wildlife sanctuary known for its huge congregations of elephants. As herds of pachyderms left the shelter of the forests and ambled towards the lake, tourists' cameras whirred and chattered. Amit was unimpressed. He impatiently quizzed everyone within earshot, 'Have you seen any frogs?' They smiled, giggled, and laughed in response. Maria's mission to interest Amit in 'normal' wildlife had failed yet again.

I couldn't help admiring the boy. He had something I will never know. I made another attempt to reassure Maria, 'At least he's interested in frogs, not snakes. Imagine what Rom's mom went through!'

She drew in her breath sharply. 'Snakes?'

A Portrait of a Grandmother

When seven-year-old Rom arrived in India, he landed in the bosom of a large family of cousins, uncles, and aunts in Bombay. The matriarch was his step-grandmother, a stern-looking, stately lady dressed in exquisite handloom saris, and numerous colourful, tinkling bangles on her arms. With typical irreverence, Rom nicknamed her Amma Doodles, and to everyone's surprise, she loved the moniker.

A decade earlier, in 1941, Amma had travelled extensively across Europe and the US. Helen Wierbun Boulter wrote in an article published in the now-defunct *The Bombay Chronicle*, 'It seemed that the Americans were obsessed with snakes. They seemed to think that in India snakes casually strolled in and out of living rooms. Their constant reference to the subject irritated her [Amma] and she repeatedly told them that she had never seen so many snakes anywhere or heard so much talk of them as in America.' As if to prove Amma right, here was her

American step-grandson talking of snakes incessantly.

Did she try to wean him away from reptiles?

'Never,' he replied laughing. 'In fact, both my mother and grandmother encouraged me. Amma brought me gifts of animal sculptures, handicrafts. There are a lot of animals in Indian art.'

One such gift was a little metal icon of Ma Ganga seated on a crocodile. Decades of worship had covered the goddess with sticky black soot from oil lamps.

One afternoon, I worked on it with tamarind pulp, a wire brush, and muscle power. Eventually, all the gunk came off, revealing the decoration on the goddess's face, her ornaments, and even the pattern of her skirt. It was a figurine of rare beauty.

'No matter how busy Amma was, she always thought of us kids,' says Rom.

In 1953, she was on a visit to Kashmir when Sheikh Abdullah presented her with the furry skin of a gorgeous snow leopard. Amma, in turn, gifted this trophy to the one person who would appreciate it—her grandson—on whose bed in boarding school it lay draped for almost seven years.

Back home for vacations, Rom frequently accompanied Amma on her travels: Mangalore, Kashmir, Sanchi. She loved a good laugh, and he was a prankster. He saw through her grave façade, and she was probably relieved to be normally treated. While Amma met artisans, Rom was off hunting snakes or fishing in nearby villages and forests. He was impressed with his grandmother's single-minded pursuit: no part of the country was too remote.

She brought their fantastic tribal art to the world.

Even though Doris, Rom's mother, was divorced from Rama, she continued to manage her mother-in-law's household until her death. She said Amma would squirrel away any nuts and snacks she found lying uneaten, only to serve them to any guests who showed up next. Doris had to perform a sleight of hand, replacing the stale, sometimes mouldy, nibbles before anyone reached for them.

During the freedom movement, Amma was scarred badly from years spent in jail, where food was inadequate and terrible. She became a compulsive hoarder.

When Rom returned from the States as a young adult, Amma and he were rarely home at the same time, although they lived in the same house. 'When we were together, she asked me lots of questions about what I was doing,' he recalls. 'But she was extremely reticent to talk about her work. And I never asked. I regret not taking more interest in what she did.'

I can see obvious signs of Amma's influence on Rom. Both worked hard to encourage traditional skills, and ensured these wares found access to the market. She was one of the pioneers of the cooperative movement in India, and it's not surprising Rom set up a cooperative of snake-catchers.

You may have guessed Amma Doodles was none other than Kamaladevi Chattopadhyaya, the force behind the resurrection of Indian handicrafts, handloom, and theatre.

Born Addicts

It was Rom's first evening at home after several weeks away. The orphaned palm civet I was rearing would just not leave him alone. It climbed up the chair and onto his shoulder, digging its sharp claws into flesh. An irritated Rom grabbed the creature and dropped it on the floor. But there was no deterring the civet. It climbed onto his shoulder with even greater urgency. Rom got rid of it again. The next time Rom grabbed it, it bit his thumb badly. I locked up the civet in another room and dressed the finger, wondering why the creature paid so much attention to Rom. Suddenly, it dawned on me: the civet wanted the glass of rum in Rom's hand. These animals are not called 'toddy cats' for nothing.

During the season, agile tappers climbed the tall palmyra trees to slice the inflorescence and hung clay pots to collect the dripping sweet sap. These pots were civet magnets. In warm weather, the sap fermented in the pot, and old-timers narrate stories of finding drunken palm civets asleep at the base of trees. Occasionally, an inebriated animal fell from a great height and died. Today, toddy tapping is prohibited in many states, leaving not just a bunch of disgruntled humans but perhaps scores of toddy cats, too.

When there is no booze to distract them, these animals live on a healthy diet of fruit and insects. In South Indian coffee plantations, toddy cats become 'coffee cats'. The animals eat the berries, digest the pulp, and poop out the beans. Their coffee bean-crammed droppings look like coarse strands of peanut brittle. In Indonesia and Philippines, plantation workers brewed coffee from these scats, after cleaning and roasting the beans, of course. The market discovered this, and now pound for pound, *kopi luwak* or civet coffee is the most expensive coffee in the world.

While the flesh of the berry doesn't have as much caffeine as the beans, I would expect even a handful of berries is probably enough to give a java jolt to these three-to-four-kilogram-heavy animals.

According to legend, the berries have enough caffeine to add a spring to the feet of goats. An observant Ethiopian goatherd got a buzz after he ate a few berries, following the example of his flock. He ran to the local seminary to share his amazing discovery, but the monks threw the beans in the fire, claiming they were the devil's handiwork. When the roasted beans released a delicious aroma, however, the monks declared they must indeed be God's gift. They raked the hard, blackened beans out of the fire, boiled them, and drank the world's first cup of coffee. That was how Ethiopians discovered coffee in the ninth century.

Another story credits a flock of hyperactive birds for leading a nomadic Yemeni Sufi mystic to the berries.

Only a fifth of the coffee crop is beans. The remaining pulp, the fleshy fruit surrounding the beans, is not fit for animal consumption because the caffeine content is too high. In experiment after experiment, animal husbandry experts found that cows, pigs, and poultry died if fed anything more than marginal amounts of the pulp. So, today, the waste is used to fertilize coffee trees.

We know caffeine is toxic to birds, pet dogs, and cats. So what is going on with our wild civets in coffee country? I assume they won't eat coffee berries until they are sick. But I'm not certain that a species, whose underage babies clamour for neat rum, would go easy on the caffeine. Even adult civets show little evidence of knowing their limits with booze. Besides, with acres and acres of attractive red berries spreading in every direction, what choice does a poor civet have? Do they chatter with each other incessantly? Does eating too many berries induce insomnia? When the berry season is over, do they get caffeine headaches?

Here's the anticlimax: it appears nobody knows!

Why did Raja die?

Raja, the elephant, frequently hung out by the side of the dirt road leading through Yala National Park to the Buddhist temple of Sithulpahuwa, Sri Lanka. He tugged at the foliage lackadaisically, an elephant minding his own business. A van crammed with pilgrims approached and the driver paused, uncertain whether to zip around the elephant or wait for him to move. Raja showed no sign of leaving, so the driver edged closer. Once the vehicle was near enough, Raja abandoned his pretence. He swung around and blocked the path. A pilgrim offered a couple of bananas. Happy with his toll, Raja moved aside and let the vehicle pass. Rom and I witnessed this scene numerous times.

Farther up the road, at the temple complex, pilgrims fed fried snacks, fruits, biscuits, and picnic leftovers to a troop of grey langurs. Sometimes, Raja would wander up to join the party. When food ran out and it was time for the pilgrims to leave, the teashop owner or a local guard would fashion a torch by setting fire to a wad of newspapers and chase the elephant away.

We love sharing food. Festivals usually culminate in a grand meal with friends and family. We invite friends home and feed them. By extension, we feed creatures, too.

Feeding animals encourages them to intrude on our space. When they approach closer, we complain of animals being a nuisance. Raja turned into a highway bully after being fed by well-meaning pilgrims. Although this story took place in Sri Lanka, Indians also feed animals such as monkeys, nilgai, and sambhar in various sanctuaries across the country. Compassion or wanting to earn divine favours drives our generosity. In reality, we play with animal lives and ours.

Barring a few exceptions, animals rarely share food. They gift morsels to their mates during courtship. Parents feed their young until they can fend for themselves. Otherwise, it is common for dominant individuals to snatch food from low-ranking members. So when we feed them, what do they make of our gesture? Wolfgang Dittus, a primatologist with the Smithsonian Primate Biology Program, says monkeys begin to see humans as subordinates. Thereafter, if any human withholds food, monkeys will grab, threaten, and turn aggressive.

We often wondered what Raja would do if a vehicle didn't stop to feed him. Rom was driving on the Sithulpahuwa route, when he saw Raja and stopped. A pilgrim van approached from the other side, with a picnic strapped to the roof rack. The driver tried to sneak past, but Raja would have none of that. He leaned on the van, wrapped his trunk around the roof, and tried to bite the roof rack.

The desperate driver tried to speed away but could get no traction. With Raja's weight bearing down on one side, two wheels lifted off the road, and the van swayed. Panic-stricken people, including an elderly woman, poured out of the vehicle. A ranger riding with Rom yelled at them to get back inside before the elephant turned on one of them. In the pandemonium, no one obeyed.

Meanwhile, Raja ripped off the rack. Bundles of food tumbled down and lay strewn across the path. As soon as the elephant moved away with the rack, the van's wheels hit the ground, and the driver lurched forward, running over the old lady.

The elephant calmly started tucking in, ignoring the chaos of children crying, people running helter-skelter and screaming. Eventually, the injured woman and her entourage got in the van and left.

When we returned to Yala after a break, Raja was missing. Since a Tamil rebel attack on the park a few years earlier, the army was a constant presence. In our absence, there had been a change of battalions. One of these newly posted soldiers had nodded off in a bunker when he was suddenly jerked awake. An elephant's trunk was sniffing the small cramped space for something to eat. Fearing for his life, the soldier fired his assault rifle.

Had Raja not been fed, he may have still been alive.

Cuckoo Mom

Early morning light filtered through the green canopy as we sipped coffee in the garden. The night's rainstorm had tossed leaves and branches everywhere. A big clean-up job awaited us. But for the moment, all was quiet, and even the birds seemed to be having a late start. The dogs lay at our feet.

Rom broke the quiet. 'The oriole nest has fallen down.'

We walked over for a look. The nest lay amidst a jumble of foliage. Rom picked up the branch and announced, 'There's a chick.'

Handing me the branch to hold out of the reach of the dogs, he went to get a rope to tie it up. The chick's posterior was sticking up. Was it still alive? When Rom returned, I asked him to set the chick upright.

'If I touch it, the chick will smell of me and the parents may reject it,' he cautioned.

'There's a hungry chick to be fed. How can they abandon it now?'

Rom turned the ugly, half-feathered chick right side up, even though its tiny talons gripped the edge of the nest tightly. We tied the branch to the tree and retreated to the house to wait and watch. The nest was slightly askew, and the branch was not in its original place.

I was beset with doubts. What if the parents didn't return? What if they rejected the chick?

Reading my mind, Rom said, 'If the parents don't start feeding the baby, you know who has to.'

I groaned.

When we lived at the Madras Crocodile Bank years ago, I had taken in an Indian cuckoo chick after a similar storm. The first lesson I learnt: chicks were gluttons. I fed it mashed fruits and insects. It was hard work being the sole provider for a hungry, demanding chick. It wanted variety and wouldn't eat the same thing again. I spent more and more time each day hunting insects.

Once the chick began to flap its wings, we cleaned up a storeroom as an enclosure. When I went to feed it that afternoon, it was perched on a blade of the ceiling fan. I pleaded with it to come down.

In response, it demanded in an even louder voice to be fed. The ladder was somewhere on the campus, and I didn't have the energy to go looking for it. So I took a cobweb duster and unceremoniously knocked the cuckoo out of its perch. This became a meal-time routine.

By the time it developed the plumage of an adult female

cuckoo, it was flying around and landing on the branches we had wired across the room. When neem trees were heavily laden with fruit, it seemed a good time to let the bird go. Besides, I wanted my freedom back.

Instead of following its nose to the nearest bunch of berries, the chick squawked and flapped from the crown of one tree to the next, following me around. Anyone who needed to find me in the Croc Bank just had to listen for that loud, raucous voice. I even dreamt of it in my sleep.

While I'd be inside a building, it perched outside and called. I couldn't climb up the tree to feed it, and neither was it going to come down. Its calls made me feel alternately guilty and exasperated. Over the course of a week, its demands grew fainter and stopped altogether. I don't know if it became independent. My only consolation is the grounds maintenance team never found a cuckoo carcass.

While I recalled that ordeal, the mother oriole arrived and, much to my relief, fed its chick.

Later that evening, Rom said, 'The leaves are already drying and soon the branch will be bare. The parents may still abandon it.'

Despite Rom's alarmist predictions, the orioles successfully reared their chick until it fledged.

Fear Factor

Are we born with a fear of snakes or do we learn it? Scientists have spent considerable effort in answering this question over the years. If humans are born fearing snakes, Rom and I must be mutants.

When I was twelve, I saw a slim, green vine snake crawling from a tree branch onto the clothesline. I ran indoors to tell my parents. To my surprise and disappointment, they were indifferent. This was my first encounter with a snake, and I expected some drama. When I went back, the snake had disappeared. I'm not alone in my lack of fear.

Some years ago, a pair of young monkeys lived in the Croc Bank. They had been captives and associated more with humans than with animals. We thought they would be ideal subjects to test. Rom let a captive python, a species that would prey on monkeys in the wild, crawl towards them. They were curious and approached the snake. The python bunched up as the monkeys advanced. When they were close enough for the snake to strike, we shouted and waved our arms to scare them away. The monkeys jumped back and looked at us with perplexity. They were babes in the woods and wouldn't have recognized a snake even if it crept up and bit them.

We weren't aware that in the 1980s, Susan Mineka of Northwestern University, Illinois, had already established that monkeys learn to fear snakes by watching others. Monkey see, monkey fear.

Rom and I have seen children watch snakes with fascination at zoos around the world. Kids are quick to spot reptiles that are sometimes well-camouflaged. Adults, however, are a sight to behold. They hold their children's hands in a white-knuckle grip as they rush past the enclosures with faces averted, or yell at kids to stay away from the glass. Many shriek hysterically and some may even faint. The adults' response seems comical, but they make a lasting impression on the kids.

In 2010, Vanessa LoBue of Rutgers University and her colleagues showed that children are acutely sensitive to images of snakes, but it takes an external trigger to develop fear. You can yell with all your might, but it's unlikely a child will learn to dread flowers or bunnies. But do the same thing with a snake, and the child is scarred for life.

Nearly twenty years ago, the Croc Bank published a poster of a king cobra. Its head was raised, exposing its golden yellow throat, and its glossy black body draped across boulders in a river bed. It looked so guileless and vulnerable that all my protective feelings rose to the fore. I gave a copy of this poster to my brother who returned it to me within a few days. He said he was too scared to have it hanging on his wall. I was puzzled. We grew up together and had the same parents, but from where did he learn to dread snakes?

I suspect the personality of the child determines his/her susceptibility to fear. Besides, parents don't have a monopoly on shaping their children's psyche; peers exert considerable influence.

Since I began living with Rom, many people I had known for a long time confessed to being snake-phobic. One friend, in particular, can't glance at a picture of one, has not seen the documentaries we make, or visited us, suspecting we have snakes running loose in the house.

Just as we learn to fear snakes, we can unlearn it. I've seen Rom convince people who are terrified of snakes to touch one. The moment they feel the dry smoothness of a snake's body, most of their fear evaporates. However, extreme phobias may take longer and considerable effort to dissipate.

I wonder if, conversely, snakes and other wild animals are born with an inherent fear of humans, or whether they learn from experience. Perhaps some even suffer from anthropophobia extreme fear of humans.

Do Snakes have Personalities?

South Indian king cobras are different from Oriya ones. Even after years in captivity at the Madras Crocodile Bank, the Oriya kings were just as feisty as they were on Day One. I dreaded the days when Rom had to feed them. The southern snakes would stalk and pounce on the dead rat that Rom dangled enticingly in front of them. The Oriya snakes, however, would bite the tongs, plants, and boulders in the enclosure, and after they ran out of things to bite, grab the rat. Sometimes, they would even look at Rom's shoes intently, although he stood still.

These temperaments are not an artefact of captivity. In the Anamalais, Tamil Nadu, one tea estate labourer brought a large snake flailing inside a gunny sack, saying it was a ratsnake. Inside was a hefty, ten-foot king cobra. Surprisingly, it had not bitten in self-defence while being caught and stuffed clumsily into the burlap.

One snake-catcher in the mangrove forest of Bhitarkanika, Orissa, wasn't so lucky; he was bitten on the nose by a wild king cobra. Even if he had been close to medical help, there is no antivenom for king cobra bite in India. Without hesitating for a moment, he swung his machete and chopped his own nose off. It is possible the snake didn't inject any venom, but had the man waited for the symptoms to develop, he might not have lived to tell the tale.

Pictures of many snake-rescuers free-handling calm king cobras from the Western Ghats circulate on social networking sites. If these heroes tried a similar stunt with the feisty Oriya ones, they wouldn't last a minute.

For centuries, snake-charmers staged mongoose-and-cobra fights. The cobras' first line of defence, to sit majestically and hiss menacingly with their heads up and hoods spread, doesn't cut any ice with mongooses. We had always assumed the quick-to-tire reptiles were no match for the agile and swift mammals.

It was only recently, when a film crew used high-speed cameras that we realized cobras strike at their tormentors from the defensive posture without opening their mouths. They are merely head-butting.

I haven't found a credible explanation for their reticence to bite.

'Venom is expensive to produce,' Rom suggested. 'Snakes may want to use it as a last resort.'

'But this is a matter of life or death,' I argued. 'If a cobra won't use its venom when a mongoose goes for its jugular, when is a good time to use it?'

Despite these broad generalizations about species' temperaments, there is variation between individual snakes.

A man showed up at our door once, holding a healthy, adult Russell's viper with his bare hands. I was still collecting my wits, when he announced he had caught a baby python.

'Put it down slowly and gently,' Rom instructed in a calm voice.

After he flipped the snake into a bag, he berated the ignorant man.

On another occasion, Rom's six-year-old son, Samir, and his partner-in-mischief, Kali, brought home a bunch of saw-scaled vipers in their little hands.

'See Dada, baby cat snakes,' said Samir.

Surprisingly and fortunately, the normally snappy vipers didn't bite either of the two kids.

Are these just instances of good fortune? Why didn't the snakes bite while being caught? Is it the easy confidence of the ignorant that protects them? Some say snakes sense nervousness and react by biting. I wonder if perhaps these individual snakes are calm by nature. Yet, many nervous and frightened cobras, Russell's vipers, and saw-scaled vipers bite tens of thousands of people every year in India.

'Do you think the personality of the individual snake determines whether an encounter with a human ends in a medical emergency?' I asked Rom.

'How do you suggest we test if a venomous snake is a Type A personality?' Rom scoffed.

Lizards of Horror

The high humidity combined with the physical exertion of the morning's film shoot left me exhausted. After lunch, I lay down on one of the wooden benches in the large, covered porch of the rangers' hut in Rinca Island, Indonesia. A loud voice made me jump.

'This is no place to sleep.' The ranger ordered, 'Get up!'

'What's the problem?' I asked as I reluctantly sat up.

'Komodo dragons.'

'But ... but this hut is on stilts.'

'A couple of months ago, a guard was sleeping there like you were. A Komodo climbed up one of the stilts and bit his arm and leg.'

When I first arrived on Rinca, I thought average-sized Komodos, less than three metres, were no more than supersized water monitor lizards, a species with which I was familiar. The difference is that the giants are fearless and powerful.

Like many island creatures, these animals are not shy.

Or perhaps they don't fear humans because they are so large. For creatures used to bringing down deer and water buffaloes, I was a pint-sized morsel. In the past thirty-five years, Komodos have killed four humans. Still, even the tall Indians and Europeans who were part of the film crew felt unsafe around these lizards. Armed with sticks, we walked in groups, constantly scanning front, back and the sides, for Komodos lying in ambush. A gigantic, carnivorous, man-eating lizard is the stuff of nightmares.

Komodos were thought to have reached their great size by feasting on 300-kilogram Stegodon elephants that lived on this group of Indonesian islands. Peculiarly, islands have a way of turning giant species like Stegodons to pygmies, and smallish species like monitor lizards to giants.

However, the tiger-sized elephants went extinct 12,000 years ago, while humans brought pigs from Sulawesi only about 7,000 years ago. The deer and buffalo came even later. In the intervening 5,000 years, Komodos managed to survive and maintain their huge sizes by hunting small prey. So did elephants really lead to the evolution of the largest lizard in the world?

In 2009, after studying fossil evidence, a team of archaeologists led by Scott Hocknull of Queensland Museum, Australia, concluded Komodos evolved in

Australia and colonized islands as far West as Java, Indonesia. Today, this race of giants has disappeared from its Australian homeland and is relegated to the Indonesian islands of Rinca, Flores, Komodo, and the two tiny islands of Gili Montang and Gili Dasami.

Fearless Komodos are scary enough. Until 40,000 years ago, lizards twice as large wandered across much of inland Australia. Called Megalania, meaning 'ancient great wanderer', the biggest ones reached seven metres in length, about 1,940 kilograms in weight, and lived off rhinoceros-sized marsupials.

Not surprisingly for creatures this size, early Aborigines were also on the menu. There was no tree a man could climb and no hole in the ground he could dig to get away from these monsters. The last Ice Age put an end to the Aborigines' nightmare.

India had a giant lizard, too. In the 19th century, two vertebrae and a thigh bone were found at an unknown location in the Siwaliks. Estimated to grow up to 3.5 metres, the lizard roamed the area 2.5 million years ago. Not only does it seem to have been rare, fortunately, it also lived in a different era from humans.

The same year Hocknull established the Australian origin of Komodo dragons, a team of venom experts led by Bryan Greig Fry, of the University of Melbourne, added a new dimension. For a long time, it was thought deadly septicemia-causing bacteria festered in the mouths of Komodos. Fry said it wasn't bacteria that disabled prey, but venom seeping from a gland located in the lizards' lower jaw. The venom disrupted blood coagulation and caused blood pressure to plummet. The quarry went into shock and lost consciousness, to be eaten at leisure by the predators.

Since Megalanias are related to Komodos and similar venomous lizards, they may have been the largest venomous vertebrates to have ever evolved.

Those poor Aborigines!

Should I Stay or Should I Go?

When I was three, a twenty-year-old girl, who used to play with me, got married and left home. I nagged my mother with questions. Where did she go? With whom will she stay? Why couldn't she stay at home? My mother explained that married women have to live with their husbands. At that time, it was the norm for grown men to live with their parents. Thereafter, whenever I got annoyed with my parents, I threatened to get married and go away to my in-laws. The warning never worked; my parents simply laughed.

A couple of years later, my brother was born. At some point, I began to fear I would be sent away from my parents, while a strange girl who married my brother would take my place. I demanded to know why only girls had to leave their homes. Why not boys? It's just how things are done, I was told.

My possible fate in a traditional Indian household was not very different from girl chimpanzees. When females reach adulthood, they are kicked out of their natal troop. They wander around until they find another troop that will take them in.

Leaving one's home and going to live with a family of strangers is a scary journey for both, women and female animals. They are deprived of support from female kin, which leaves them vulnerable to male, and female aggression. Many animals lose their lives in the process. Neighbouring troops may react violently to trespassers on their territory. If the neighbours don't get you, predators will.

Finding food in a strange area is a challenge, and the threat of starvation imminent. Women spend their married lives among people to whom they are not genetically related. Their survival and well-being depend on being accepted.

The purpose of leaving home and family is to avoid inbreeding, competing with blood relatives, and to seek better pastures. Why should one gender leave the comfort of its home and take on the burden of keeping the species fit, at risk to its own life? Does the way our family life is organized determine which sex disperses?

Several males and females live together in macaque troops, and pubescent males typically move out. Orangutans are solitary, and sons disperse while daughters live close-by. Teenage males leave gelada harems. But in gorilla harems, young females set out to join another harem. Chimpanzee groups are similar to macaques, but daughters leave. In nominally monogamous pairs of hoolock gibbons, offspring of both sexes leave their parents' home. There seems to be no pattern. Besides, our family structures bear little resemblance to chimp troops, gorilla harems, or, for that matter, to lone orangutans.

One thing seemed certain: if my brother and I belonged to any of the vast majority of non-human primate societies, he would have to find another troop, while I stayed at home. This arrangement makes the best reproductive sense for females because they have family support and shelter. Their sisters, mothers, and aunts help with baby-rearing duties. Daughters inherit hierarchical position in the troop without having to jostle for it. I wished Indians were like these 'males, go away' monkeys.

I took another stab at approaching the question. Was dispersal related to making babies? In macaque society, low-ranking males stand little chance of passing on their genes, while high-ranking ones father most of the next generation. Males at the bottom of the ladder have a better chance of reproducing when they leave their troops and join others. However, whether females rank low or high, they are assured of making babies and so they stay. That is one theoretical explanation for the dispersal of males. But macaque society isn't rigid. Some silly females forsake their families and join other troops. Why would they do that?

In the 1980s, Rauf Ali, a primatologist who studied bonnet macaques in Kalakkad-Mundanthurai Tiger Reserve, Tamil Nadu, reported females flee their parental homes. This was unheard-of in macaque society. More recently, Anindya Sinha, studying the species in Bandipur Tiger Reserve, Karnataka, also found female macaques leaving their natal troops.

In Bandipur, tourists routinely feed monkeys. Sinha found that when there is a shortage of natural food in the forest, human handouts cause aggression between monkeys to rise five-fold. One group of subordinate females that was harassed by high-ranking members split from the troop. A single male took over this band of rebels, a previously unheard-of occurrence. The new lord of the harem kept other males from approaching his ladies. But female macaques mate with more than one male. Given this lack of choice in mates, the females left one by one and joined other troops.

In another instance, two males appeared on the periphery of another troop Sinha was observing. Attracted to the strangers, a female eloped, even abandoning her six-month-old offspring. She followed her new paramours to the edge of a neighbouring troop's territory and hung around for a couple of days. Then she returned to her own troop, picked up her baby, and left to join the neighbours.

Male macaques are no less aggravating. Instead of leaving their natal troops with no exceptions made, some choose to stay home. Among rhesus and Japanese macaques, occasionally, sons of dominant females stay with their mommies even after reaching adulthood. Achieving high status appears to be a disincentive for leaving. Apparently, the dreaded inbreeding issue doesn't bother these boys.

These fascinating exceptions to the rule didn't answer my question: how does a species as a whole decide which sex leaves home?

I started from scratch again. Irrespective of the varied

family structures among the African great apes, be they gorillas, chimps, or bonobos, females appear to be the dispersing sex. And since we are most closely related to them, does it all come down to evolutionary roots? That would mean the boys-stay-home tendency had to date back more than 8 million years, before our lineages split. Surely, if it had such deep evolutionary roots, there wouldn't be so much flexibility.

When I talked about my confusion with Rauf Ali, he chuckled as he said, 'We don't really know if there is a universal species-wide rule. When I first began studying macaques, if a male went missing, primatologists would say, "Male dispersed." If a female disappeared, they noted, "Female died." It's only now, with more detailed studies, we find primate society is much more complex.'

In 1984, Ali wrote a seminal paper with his colleague, Jim Moore of Harvard University, challenging the concept of the 'dispersing sex'. They declared there was none, and either sex could disperse.

Macaques aren't the only nonconformists. Despite popular belief, recent DNA analysis of orangutans in some populations reveals that males and females move the same distance from their mothers. Among gorillas, it now emerges that girls may not be the only dispersing sex. Both sexes disperse, while girls move farther than boys. Chimps are the only rigid ape society where the girls invariably leave. But there appear to be exceptions even here. Moore and Ali cite instances of female chimps that returned to their natal troop after brief absences.

'Who leaves is resource-driven,' said Anindya Sinha. 'And the resource may be food or mates.'

Is this true for humans, too? In a typically patrilineal human society, sons inherit property and support their parents in old age. Such cultures look down upon sons who move in with their in-laws. Several Indian languages use a disdainful term for this, such as *gharjamai* in Hindi or *veettoda mapillai* in Tamil.

Even in other patrilineal systems such as polygyny with multiple wives and polyandry with multiple husbands, sons inherit property and daughters leave.

However, not all Indians are patrilineal.

Traditionally, women of these communities—the Nair and Mappila of Kerala, the Khasi and Garo of Meghalaya, and the Nicobarese of the Nicobar Islands—stay at their parents' homes and inherit property. S. Anvar, a chronicler of South Indian Muslim heritage, notes Marakkayar Muslims of coastal Tamil Nadu follow the same system, too. Why do some communities allow women to stay in their birth home while others don't?

If it's all to do with inheritance, what do nomadic hunter-gatherers do? After all, they have few possessions to bequeath.

The Irula, here in Tamil Nadu, have been forced to settle down over the years, but they haven't given up their hunter-gatherer ways entirely. When Kali, an Irula tribal who works with us, got married, he lived with his wife's family for a while. Then he moved to his widowed mother's settlement. When she remarried, Kali and his wife lived with his mother and stepfather's family for some time. At other times, the couple lived with the wife's sister, aunts, uncles, and brothers-in-law. If we had to pick up Kali before going on a hike, we had to first find out his current residence. Like many other tropical foraging communities, Kali and his wife didn't move away from their parents permanently. I couldn't find a comparable primate society.

If this is a reflection of the family life of early humans, then the boys-stay-and-girls-leave tradition developed later, when we made the shift from nomadic foraging to animal husbandry and agriculture, about 10,000 years ago.

A team of anthropologists led by Kim Hill of Arizona State University says the level of cooperation and group organization among our hunter-gatherer forebears is the reason for the exceptional success of mankind.

When members of early hunting-and-gathering humans travelled between groups, new ideas and innovations travelled with them and spread to a wide network of people. Such cultural exchanges gave our ancestors an edge over other primates and rival human species.

Although some members of a hunter-gatherer band were related by blood or marriage, several were unrelated to each other. Yet, they all cooperated. No other primate appears to collaborate with unrelated individuals in hunting, gathering, sharing food, and rearing children. This behaviour is unprecedented in the animal world.

According to a theory proposed by economist Brishti Guha, women stay home and till the land in societies that are at war. Besides, the Mappila and Marakkayar are maritime tradesmen, while the Nicobarese are hunters. In all these cases, women stay with their parents and kin since their husbands are absent for long periods of time. The flip side of the situation is the husbands have no way of ascertaining the paternity of their wives' children. Rather than invest in a child with whom they may share no genes, they invest in their sisters' children with whom they definitely share some genetic affinity. Therefore, wealth passes through women in such communities.

If women live in their in-laws' households, paternity of children is not in doubt. That's why girls are made to leave their parental homes. In such communities, assets are handed down father to son. This is not the last word on the subject and we can look forward to many other theories in the future.

It seems ironic that we established our uniqueness as humans by evolving an exceptional collaborative lifestyle, but in dealing with property and assets, we relapsed into a non-human primate manner of dealing with relationships.

Once I became independent, I fledged from my parents' nest. A few years later, my brother went halfway across the world, married, and settled down. Like urban, nuclear families everywhere, both sexes emigrated.

A few years after Rom and I moved to our farm, an interesting thing happened.

My parents dispersed—they came to live with Rom and me.

Snake Oil Merchants

You'd be forgiven for thinking our snakes had udders instead of fangs. No other country in the world seizes as much illegal snake venom as India. In Jalpaiguri, West Bengal, in October 2016, forest officials claimed they had arrested four for smuggling contraband venom worth £ 30 million (Rs. 245 crores).

A common widespread venomous snake that produces copious amounts of venom is the spectacled cobra. Its venom sells for $ 150 (Rs. 10,000) per gram on the international market. King cobras produce even more venom, priced at $ 120 a gram.

Officials claim the haul was worth a fantastic Rs. 245 crore. *The Telegraph* put a more conservative value at Rs. 175 crores. You can buy more than 175 kilograms of legal venom for the lower sum. But they seized only 10 kilograms in five fancy bulletproof jars. (Why on earth does venom need to be in bulletproof containers?) The officials want us to believe a gram of this spurious venom is worth Rs.

1,75,000. No venom from an Indian snake is that expensive. Since smugglers cannot guarantee the authenticity of their product, the legal availability of venom ought to drive the price way down.

Most consignments of confiscated venom are in liquid form, and therefore not even worth a paisa. That's because, like any other bodily fluid, venom starts rotting as soon as it leaves the snake's body. It has to be instantly frozen or freeze-dried to a powder.

Besides, it takes hundreds of king cobras to produce a litre of venom. It is impossible for a clandestine backyard operation to amass such a quantity. But these little details didn't prevent the police from making wild claims about the value of the venom.

In the Jalpaiguri case, officials say the venom was for medicinal purposes and manufacture of antivenom. Firstly, antivenom manufacturers don't need kilograms of venom to produce antivenom. Secondly, they don't buy any random venom; they need to know the particular species of snake to which the venom belongs. Neither do they buy from dubious sources at Crown Jewel-prices. The price of antivenom is under Rs. 1,000 a vial. If manufacturers had to buy raw material at Rs. 1,75,000 a gram, they couldn't afford to sell antivenom at throwaway prices.

They buy from known suppliers who guarantee the product. One such organization is the Irula Snake Catchers' Cooperative that took nearly thirty-five years and 35,000 cobras to produce 10 kilograms of cobra venom.

So clearly, the black market venom wasn't intended for any legitimate use.

In 2011, the police claimed that snake venom was mixed

with narcotics for 'an extra kick'. More than twenty years ago, we heard rumours of addas—meeting places where people gather to smoke dope or other illicit substances—in Kolkata where addicts got cobras to bite their tongues. When we enquired in that city, we were told to look in Mumbai; when we asked there, it was somewhere else. The story even made it internationally to *The National Enquirer*. To Rom's chagrin, a photograph of him milking a cobra was the accompanying illustration.

In 2012, an official from the Narcotics Control Bureau added another twist to the story. He said revellers at rave parties add a pinch of dry cobra venom to their drinks 'to enhance sensation and boost energy' so they can dance for longer hours.

Snakes didn't evolve venom to let their prey have happy hours before dining on them. Instead, they custom-produce venom, a lethal combination of enzymes and toxins, to kill specific prey in seconds. Cobra venom attacks the nervous system, leading to paralysis. Viper venom damages tissue and causes blood to flow freely.

Of the one million snakebites that occur in India every year, about 50,000 citizens lose their lives. Not one patient reported getting high. The experience appears to be invariably traumatizing.

Venom has to be injected into the bloodstream to have an effect. If you swallow it, stomach acids destroy it and you'll experience nothing as long as you have no ulcers.

'It's possible to get a high from venom injected into your body,' says Bryan Grieg Fry, Head of the Venom Evolutionary Laboratory at University of Queensland, Australia. 'I had that feeling when I was bitten by a death adder. But that's about when your lungs fail. Sadly, the people on all sides of this farce have it all wrong. Any cobra venom delivered the way they are saying it is would have no effect.'

Despite overwhelming evidence to the contrary, authorities repeat the ridiculous myth that venom gives people a high.

It's not just snake venom that seems to have a thriving underground market. A couple of years ago, press reports claimed red sand boas were being illegally traded for lakhs of rupees each. Soon, there were suppliers from every southern state eagerly looking for buyers. Villagers who knew of our interest in snakes sought our help in making their fortunes.

We couldn't fathom who would be interested in a lethargic, uncharismatic species at such high prices and why. The authorities also seemed clueless, speculating on a wide range of options—aphrodisiacs, get-rich talismans, food, medicine, and black magic.

Unfortunately, in this case, these snakes are taken from the wild and held in captivity until the poachers can find buyers. Since some news reports claimed the snakes are sold by weight, some activists say the reptiles are frequently force-fed metal ball bearings. Just when I think I've heard it all, other reports make the fantastic claim that these burrowing snakes accumulate rare, invaluable iridium in their scales. Why don't earthworms?

If the so-called venom is not for antivenom, then what else is it used for? *The Telegraph* says it may be destined for the manufacture of traditional Chinese medicine, presumably in China. Why would the Chinese, who do a roaring business in snake meat and blood, procure venom that makes its way through Bangladesh and India? After all, Chinese cobra venom is cheaper, selling at $ 68 a gram. Even if they need large quantities, they can easily import it directly.

To add intrigue to the story, officials of the forest department claim the venom came from France. The evidence? The sticker of a purported French venom supplier on the jars. In a similar case in 2015, officials found 'Made in France' labels on the jars. How much effort does it take to stick a label to impress a prospective buyer?

Typically, venom suppliers sell venom for pharmaceutical use, in quantities varying between 10 milligrams and 10 grams. They securely package it in small pharmaceutical vials, not in ornate 'bulletproof' jars.

Assuming there was such a facility in France and the venom did come from there, it's not a crime to have it in one's possession in India. The Indian Wildlife Protection Act does not extend jurisdiction to non-Indian species, says Jose Louies, Head of Enforcement and Law, Wildlife Trust of India (WTI).

How do we even know the powder in the jars is venom?

Cocaine sells for only $ 200 a gram. Let's assume dealers see the officials' claim that venom sells for Rs. 1,75,000 a gram. They can claim their *maal*—merchandise—is snake venom and mark up the price nearly twenty times. Cocaine is one of many venom look-alikes. The white powder could be anything from dandruff to bleaching powder.

Who knows what these guys sell? Desperate drug abusers in search of the next high are idiotic enough to swallow any rubbish peddled by dealers.

The illegal trade in wildlife and purported wildlife products is driven in no small measure by the authorities quoting fantastic prices, giving the impression there's a killing to be made. Anyone out to make a quick buck wants in. If they have a source for snake venom, they might adulterate it with something else to make up the bulk. In two instances, the substance tested appeared to have cobra venom. 'One case was detected at Cochin Airport, and the other in Kasaragod district,' says Avinash Basker, Head of the legal programme, Wildlife Protection Society of India (WPSI). 'Both convictions occurred in 2013.'

If the scamsters aren't able to get their hands on venom, any white powder would do. They might think … how is a gullible buyer going to test it in some sleazy hotel room anyway. If they find a sucker, they've got it made. If not, there's not much to lose. Of course, they could get caught peddling the stuff to undercover officials.

Although such news reports make good copy—pots of money, exotic substance, bulletproof jars, officers with automatic weapons, and so-called criminals wearing pillowcases over their heads notwithstanding—the cases unravel quickly.

'First, the prosecution has to establish that the seized material is snake venom or derivatives from snake venom,' says Louies. Then it has to prove which Indian species was milked to produce this venom. Only then can the case make it through the court.

Selling fake wildlife products is not a new phenomenon.

Sale of cow hides painted with tiger stripes has been going on for a long time. 'There is no provision of the WLPA [wildife act] that applies to cow skins,' says Basker. 'The WLPA only applies to the species and their derivatives listed in its schedules.' Similarly, a suspect selling some white powder that he calls venom cannot be prosecuted under wildlife laws. But the police do file charges of cheating in such cases, says Tito Joseph, programme manager, WPSI.

If Indian law enforcement is really serious about curbing this illicit business, it shouldn't put an unrealistic value on untested substances said to come from wild species. And for the sake of its own credibility, it should stop issuing press releases before testing the substances. If it waited for the test results, it would find it has nothing to crow about, nor would it create snake oil merchants.

The Poop of the Matter

Koko, our puppy, came running to greet me, and I bent down to scoop her up. But I recoiled at the last minute. Her breath stank of faeces. I scolded her whenever I caught her eating poop, but she wouldn't desist. So I followed her whenever she went out to do her job and poured vinegar over the poop. I thought that would solve the problem. But I continued to get that disgusting whiff on her breath. Was she eating other dogs' business? I poured vinegar on all the droppings I could find.

'Koko must be suffering from mineral deficiency,' the vet said.

She prescribed a supplement, but the puppy persisted in seeking a poop fix. Perhaps vinegar wasn't distasteful enough, so I sprinkled chilli powder. Either Koko was somehow finding ungarnished poop or she was immune to chilli powder.

Not only is poop appealing to some animals, but it can also make the difference between life and death.

About twenty years ago, a clutch of green iguanas hatched for the first time at the Madras Crocodile Bank. No matter what herpetologist Farida Tampal fed them, they refused to eat. We became concerned as the hatchlings lost condition. Rom and Farida pored over books on iguana care, and wrote to specialists in the States and Europe. Someone suggested letting the hatchling iguanas taste their mother's faeces.

The hatchlings didn't merely taste mamma's poop; they gobbled it up as if it was a delicacy. There were no more feeding problems. Apparently, iguanas hatch from eggs without any gut flora or bacteria vital for digestion. By eating mamma's excreta, they inoculate themselves with a culture of bacteria that lasts for their lifetime.

Since then, I've discovered many babies like rat pups, koala joeys, foals, and elephant and hippo calves need an inoculation of their mothers' gut bacteria. Besides microorganisms, a rat mamma's droppings are rich in deoxycholic acid that is essential for the development of nerves, and for fighting infections.

Other creatures, such as hares and rabbits, are regular poop-eaters. Jonah, a baby black-naped hare, came to live with us after his mother was killed by a predator.

He produced soft, moist, tan-coloured pellets and hard, dry, black ones. He ate most of the soft pellets but didn't touch the others. Biologists say when these creatures are prevented from eating their poop, they lose weight and become anaemic.

Eating poop seems to be a peculiarly vegetarian adaptation. Some herbivores like cows have multi-chambered stomachs to break down plant cellulose, while hares have simple digestive systems. Cows chew the cud, and hares eat poop.

Some animals' poop is other animals' manna. Pigs seem to love faeces of any kind. And then there are dung beetles that live solely on excreta.

Naturally, my next question was: from where do we get our gut flora. Some scientists suggest we are born with them, and others say we gulp some while popping out of our mothers' birth canals. In case of caesarian births, bacteria are transmitted when adults fondle and kiss us as babies.

Later in life, should these micro-organisms get nuked by antibiotics, our stomachs can be colonized by a nasty bacterium, *Clostridium difficile*, which causes severe chronic diarrhoea, and even death. The condition is now being successfully treated by faecal bacteriotherapy, transferring gut flora from a healthy person to the patient's colon. It sounds like a disgusting, far-out medical fad, but more and more case histories are being published in respected journals such as the *Journal of Clinical Gastroenterology*.

Koko eventually stopped eating dog poop, but a new problem arose. When monkeys roost anywhere on the farm overnight, all the dogs make a beeline for the spot the following morning and gobble up the droppings. Our dogs have plenty of gut flora and are well-fed. What could be so appetizing about stinky, brown faecal matter? Then I read that monkey poop is rich in Vitamin B-12. Could that explain the gastronomic attraction?

Or are our dogs pigs reincarnate?

Life in A Zoo

Rom and I sit in front of the computer, looking at the newly scanned images of old photographs. When pictures of our life at the Madras Crocodile Bank in the early 1990s light up the screen, old memories rush up from deep recesses. Meanwhile, Cyclone Nilam is revving up its centrifugal engine offshore, bringing steady rain and cold, turbulent wind.

A picture of me as a young woman leaning back against a tree. I was sitting on a rise overlooking a pond. It was early morning, and out of the camera frame were our mugs of hot tea. Young *rohu* and *catla* fish hung around in shoals patiently waiting to be fed. But that morning, Rom was intent on taking pictures. We had recently fallen in love. In the photograph, my face is clear. I was unaware that a few months later, our relationship would go into a tailspin.

It was our ritual to drink tea by the pond while feeding fish or to be on the beach before sunrise, hoping a school of dolphins would come by. Occasionally, a catamaran pulled up. Men shouted rhythmically and in unison as they dragged the heavy nets ashore. Sometimes rays, squids, and sea snakes lay motionless among the flip-flopping fish. After buying a bunch of fish for lunch, we trotted over the hot sand for the shelter of Croc Bank.

Some memories arise unbidden by images, for instance, waking up to the steady metronome of waves crashing ashore; I called it the earth's heartbeat. Then, the ceaseless sound was an addictive lullaby. If I were to spend a night at the Croc Bank today, many years after we moved away, the roar of the waves would keep me awake.

A group of people cleaning a croc enclosure. Young women from the village across the road came to work with a string of jasmine flowers tucked in their braids. The sand muffled the tinkling of their silver anklets. The women tucked their colourful nylon saris higher before leaping over the enclosure walls. Round-bellied Ganga or sprightly Paindy acted as bodyguards, armed with nothing more than a casuarina pole to keep the toothy crocodiles at bay. The women swept up crocodile dung deftly into large aluminium baskets. I can't see their faces, but I can guess who they are. Most of them are mothers of teenage children now.

I am standing at a table in the office, printing faxes and letters. I remember being impatient with Rom that morning as he was getting in my way. I was trying to beat the 9 a.m. deadline, when two men set off in opposite directions. One went to Madras city to do our shopping, while another went to Mahabalipuram to send faxes and pick up mail from the post office. If we needed anything, we tore off a sheet from a pad of printed requisition slips and wrote down what we wanted, how many, from which shop, and which account would pay for it. One morning, a researcher, fed up with washing her laundry by hand, scrawled 'washing machine' on a slip. Clothes are hand-washed to this day.

Rom standing outside the office, speaking on the phone; the cord snaking through the window bars. There were no telephones at the Croc Bank for a long while. Mobile phones were a few years away. Riding pillion and hugging Rom, as he gunned the motorbike down the empty strip of coastal road for 14 kilometres in the midday sun to make a phone call is a fond memory.

Then landline phones arrived, and they were a nuisance. There seemed to be an unwritten rule that the person needed on the phone would be nowhere near at hand. Many times a day, I ran down the length of Croc Bank to fetch the person.

These days, I catch myself before I spout off like an old crone, 'You people don't know what it was like without walkie-talkies and mobile phones.'

In one of the photographs, I spot Rom's HAM radio call sign, VU2WIT, scrawled on the wall. Rom got a radio license to communicate with Alok Mallik, who managed Croc Bank's station in the Andaman Islands. Occasionally, Rom would turn on the instrument and eavesdrop on conversations. I don't recall hearing him say anything, not even to Alok. One night, a lightning bolt hit the antenna and fried the radio.

In the photograph, I see the edge of the wooden cassette shelves against one wall. The office always had rock 'n' roll playing on an automobile tape recorder because, when it reached the end of one side, it would automatically play the other side. Frequently, the same tape played over and over for hours before someone popped another in.

Whenever Rom visited his brother in New York, he recorded a radio station that played music all day long on numerous tapes. Once home, he painstakingly edited out the advertisements and DJ chatter, and we had cassettes of shuffled music labelled Mix 1, 2, 3 and so on. Music was a necessity for Rom to function, and our radio stations didn't measure up.

Rom holds a baby gharial in the nursery. When drawing up film budgets became tedious, we had plenty of outdoor work. There were feeding and cleaning chores in the croc nursery, plants to be replaced in enclosures, seeds to be planted in the plant nursery, vegetables to be chopped for tortoises, and leaves and flowers picked for iguanas. If there was any research or animal work going on, I recorded it on video and stills.

Rom and I bob in the ocean, waving our hands. On hot afternoons, we fought the rough currents in a bid to cool off. But when the sea was calm, we floated with our eyes shut against the brilliant sun. We did have to make sure the current wasn't taking us farther down the coast. If it did, we'd have to walk back on the hot sands, and that was no fun. Besides us, there wouldn't be a soul on the beach.

A hundred little pinpoints of light gleam out of the darkness. Croc eyes. It was usually dark when we left the office, and in the torchlight, hundreds of croc eyes reflected back at us like stars. This was the best time at the Bank, when there were no visitors or workers. Staff and researchers had retired to their own homes elsewhere on the grounds. There was just Rom, me, and hundreds of crocodiles. The buzzing of tree crickets was punctuated by a croc coughing, one sliding into the water, or a minor scuffle. The magic lasted until clouds of whining mosquitoes sent us fleeing.

Later, we nursed our drinks on the beach, and watched the lights of trawlers on the horizon. Rom taught me the names of constellations. I repeated what I had learnt to a guest who knew better, and it was soon clear Rom had been making it all up. That ended our astronomy lessons, although Rom still proclaims his expertise.

My memories are vivid, but those quiet, private moments were few. Rom travelled most of the time, and when he was home, I had to surrender him to colleagues.

While I enjoyed living at the Croc Bank, I also remember aching to get away. It was an island of civilization back then, surrounded by miles of casuarina plantations and occasional holiday homes. We only had other staff for company. We were in each other's homes and lives much more than was healthy. Even the best friendships could dissolve in such a fishbowl. Some did and brought grief.

When I slowly return to the present, it takes me a moment to realize I'm no longer at the Croc Bank; the power has long since gone off, and I'm staring out the window without seeing. It isn't the roar of crashing waves I hear, but Cyclone Nilam making landfall.

The High Price of Sex

How would a nubile female king cobra seduce a potential mate without becoming prey? After all, king cobras are snake-eaters, and cannibalism is a distinct possibility.

All female snakes give off a special scent that attracts males of their kind during the breeding season. But king cobra girls have another trick: they flash a golden yellow chevron-shaped marking on the backs of their heads by flaring their hoods. Ratsnakes, king cobras' staple diet, don't have this mark, nor do they have hoods. Only a blind and anosmic (no sense of smell) male king cobra would confuse his squeeze for a meal.

It helps that the males of many snake species starve when they go looking for sex. However, at the Madras Crocodile Bank, captive male king cobras did not lose appetite. They ate just as well as any other time of the year. We don't know whether studs in the wild fast during the breeding season.

In 2008, field assistants of the king cobra research project were called to remove a snake from a farmer's courtyard in Agumbe, Karnataka. They discovered two king cobras hiding in a hole under a tree buttress. The assistants convinced the farmer to leave the creatures alone and reassured him by keeping watch from afar. It was late in the breeding season, and for three weeks, the snakes had a regular routine of basking, mating, and hiding.

One day, the honeymoon turned into a horror show without warning. The 11-foot-large male suddenly clamped his jaws around the eight-foot-long female's slender neck. She twisted and struggled, but he had her in a bulldog grip. Her throat ripped and blood gushed out. She would not die easily. Perhaps she was immune to his venom. She fought for her life for forty-five minutes and lost.

It was hard to watch the video recording of this tragedy. I covered my face with my hands and listened to the assistants sobbing on the sound track.

When I looked again, the male was swallowing the female's lifeless body. He reached her baby bump, regurgitated, and crawled away. For many minutes after the screen went blank, we sat shell-shocked. Some of us had tears streaming down our cheeks.

One assistant said ten days before the tragic incident, another male king cobra had shown up. The two males had fought and the defeated one crawled away. The animals weren't marked as they weren't part of the research project. So the assistants didn't know who won. Even the video recording was no help as the snakes disappeared under bushes frequently. Was the murderer the new or old male?

Someone suggested perhaps the female had mated with the defeated male, and hence the victor killed her. But why canoodle for ten days before killing her?

Male spiders, scorpions, and praying mantids pay with their lives for sex. Reverse sexual cannibalism is rarer, practised by a few arachnids and crustaceans. I found only one case of sexual cannibalism in vertebrates, and it was another snake. Some female green anacondas eat one of their smaller suitors as a last meal before fasting through their seven-month pregnancies.

Did the male king cobra think she was a ratsnake? Before he grabbed the female's throat, he had made courtship overtures, and she had responded appropriately.

Did the male king cobra get his feeding and mating cues mixed up? Then why throw up? King cobras eat stout snakes like pythons. The female's belly bulge was not large enough to choke. Maybe this was just a rare aberration, we consoled each other.

A couple of weeks after this horrendous incident, one of the female king cobras in Rom's research project was found dead. The front part was rotten, as if a male had swallowed her and puked. She had a flat tummy; no eggs. Were male king cobras psychopaths?

We don't know. Soon afterwards, the research project terminated.

If I could offer advice to female king cobras, I would say: mate and run.

To Drive an Elephant

In 2007, I travelled around the country to learn about deterring elephants from farmlands. Many methods were being tested, such as erecting electric fences, growing patchouli instead of rice, and stringing chilli-paste-smeared ropes around fields. One organization championed driving elephants across the landscape into forests. It was described as a major operation involving captive and trained kumki elephants and lots of people, mostly men.

'Who decides what path the drive will take?' I asked one of the staff.

'The forest department officials.'

The phone rang. A bull elephant was in the middle of a tea estate and had to be driven. We arrived at the scene at the same time as the forest officials. The elephant rose like a large boulder above the low tea bushes.

'So, which way are you going to drive it?' I asked a forest official.

He jerked his chin toward the wild elephant and said, 'The guards will decide.'

I followed his gaze. Two kumki elephants, with mahouts sitting astride them, were walking toward the wild elephant, followed by two forest guards on foot. I didn't know what to expect. Nobody had maps, there was no discussion of roles, nor contingency plans made.

Suddenly, the large tame kumki charged at the smaller, wild bull and their foreheads collided in a cloud of dust. The latter tottered backwards. The large bull rammed him again and bit the wild animal's trunk and head. 'Is this done to intimidate the wild elephant?' I asked the official.

He didn't answer. Instead, he tersely barked orders in a language I didn't understand into his radio. Everyone seemed tense.

The mahout astride the large kumki was shouting, and his legs were frantically kicking the elephant behind the ears. Was he goading his elephant to attack or retreat? Everyone was shouting, including the officials standing next to me. I realized they wanted the tame elephant to stop attacking, but the animal wouldn't obey. Then one of the officials shot his rifle in the air a couple of times. Finally, the tame kumki stopped its assault, and the wild bull began walking rapidly towards us, pursued by the two tame elephants and guards. The drive had begun.

The forest officials said we should go ahead and warn people. When we arrived at a major road, there was already a crowd of about 300 people watching the drive. There were no megaphones or a public address system of any kind. Forget crowd control, we joined the bystanders. The wild bull came close to the road, saw the people, and stopped. He smashed a nearby wall topped with broken glass, and disappeared inside a vast compound.

It was an army encampment. The forest officials would have to go all the way around, and get permission to enter the camp before resuming the drive. When nothing happened for a couple of hours, I called it a day.

Later, I interviewed the staff of another NGO working in the area. 'During a drive, who makes the decisions?' I asked.

'The mahouts. The situation changes so fast, only they can decide what needs to be done, and how.'

'Not the guards?' I asked, wanting to be sure.

'No. The mahouts are on top of their elephants. They can see the terrain and action. Guards are on foot.'

As the responsibility of the drive moved down the hierarchy, I couldn't be sure if it indeed stopped with the mahouts. But there was no one else below them.

A couple of days later, I met a senior official of the first organization.

'You know an amazing thing about these elephant drives? It's not people who make the decisions; it's the kumkis,' he said. 'They hear and understand the infrasound communications between wild elephants. And the kumkis decide the best course of action.'

I wonder whether the kumkis would have passed the buck to someone else, if they could.

The Rat-trappers

The trap had sprung and the bait was gone. 'The rat got away again,' I yelled from the kitchen. I heard Rom's muffled groan in response. He was still in bed as dawn had not yet broken. For at least ten days in a row, the rat managed to gnaw away the bait and escape the slamming spring-loaded bow.

When setting rat traps, Rom went into hunting mode. 'You have to think like a rat to get it,' he has often instructed me. He smeared cheese all over the wooden base of the trap, fastened a peanut with string to the bait holder, and stuck a gob of peanut butter to it firmly. It was a sure way of getting the quarry. Until now.

The people who make rat catching an art form are the tribal people living in these parts: the *Irula* and *Korava*. Parrys is one of the busiest and most congested parts of Chennai city. At night, the Korava prowl through the empty alleys, watched suspiciously by packs of yapping stray dogs. Should a bandicoot be seen scooting, *whack*! A perfectly aimed shot to the head and the bandicoot writhes in its death throes. The Korava weapon of choice is a simple catapult. Shop owners who suffer rodent damage hire the tribesmen to rid them of the pests. The following morning, the hunters are paid per killed animal.

The Irula are more hands-on in their approach. When they find a rat burrow in a rice field, they plug all the exits, save one. They take an earthen pot with a hole, the size of a one-rupee coin, punched through the bottom, fill the pot with green leaves, and set the leaves on fire. They place the mouth of the pot flush against the burrow entry and blow through the pot's hole. After the smoke has filled every underground chamber, they excavate the burrow and pull out all the asphyxiated rats. In the case of field rats, there might be a stockpile of grain inside the burrow as a bonus.

At sunset, the Irula pile up dry thorns in a fallow field and barbeque the rats. The fur is singed and removed along with the guts, and the rest roasted. Children vie for the crunchy tails and feet. Some of you may recoil in disgust, but these are clean, field rats grown fat on rice grain. The Irula will not eat filthy bandicoots or smelly house rats. Those are killed and discarded.

In the mid-1980s, with a grant from the Department of Science and Technology, Rom conducted a pilot study to prove the cost-effectiveness of employing the Irula as rodent pest controllers. In a short period of eight months, close to 1,000 Irula caught about 2,40,000 rats from 500 acres of farmland and recovered five tonnes of grain.

Comparatively, the commercial pest control companies set out poison baits and can only roughly estimate the number of rodents they kill since rats die inside burrows. There is no estimate of the numbers that escape without eating a lethal dose. This method also causes unintentional deaths of mammals and reptiles that may consume either the baits or poisoned rats. Rom estimated the Irula were fifteen times more cost-effective than poison baits.

Recently, Rom requested the district collector to make rat catching one of the jobs provided under the National Rural Employment Guarantee Scheme. Although the official agreed with Rom's rationale, he demurred saying it would be a public relations disaster. 'Government makes poor tribals catch rats for a living' doesn't make the administration look nice. And so Irula skills continue to go unappreciated and under-utilized.

Back at home, when the rat triggered the trap once again and escaped, Rom turned the trap this way and that and scratched his head. I might have to call the Irula since rats have learnt to outwit Rom and his trap.

I sang softly, 'That's right, the rat is … uh … smarter.' (Sorry, Harry Belafonte!)

Whitaker and Boas

Rom's sons aren't the only ones to share his name. A species of snake does, too: Whitaker's sand boa. For years prior to the snake's christening, many dismissed it as a hybrid. Its irregular blotches reminiscent of the common sand boa are faintly visible, and the whole snake is of a reddish hue, much like the red sand boa. Others thought it was a variant of one of the two other Indian sand boas. But Rom recognized it as a unique species, as it was found only in the Western Ghats. There was no reason why a hybrid of two widespread species should have a restricted range. Hence, the snake was named after Rom by colleague Indraneil Das.

'What a snake to have named after me! It looks like dog sh*t,' Rom often grumbled. The snake is so placid when it lies coiled in your hands ... not only does it look uncannily like dog poo, it even acts like it. The boa neither bites nor does it try to escape. I guess Rom wants a snake with more oomph, like a cobra or krait, to bear his name.

We visited a snake park in Kerala. The signboard above the boa enclosure read 'Whitaker's sad boa'. We alerted the keeper to the typo. Months later, we were travelling through the same town and stopped at the park. The name on the signboard had been changed, but read 'Whitaker and boa'. The font size of the whole name would have to be re-sized in order to correct it. We haven't visited the place since. For all we know, visitors may still be looking for the elusive Whitaker in that exhibit.

Not much is known about the species, but we expected it to behave like its relatives, the other two burrowing sand boas. However, during our frequent visits to the Western Ghats, we found it in unlikely places: in trees and on roofs of houses. Not once or twice, but several times. That's unusual, for sand boas are earthbound snakes.

'Your sand boa climbs trees. How cool is that!' I mollified Rom.

Months after we moved to our farm, we realized we hadn't seen a single common sand boa, a related species. The ground was hard clay and as dense as concrete for most of the year. No snake could burrow through it unless it wielded a jackhammer.

'Sand boas don't always burrow,' Rom said. 'They could also use rat burrows.'

Still, there was no sign of the species.

Then what we discovered surprised us. The long, curved, locally-made terracotta roof tiles arranged in interlocking rows kept the verandah cool. But they were also a perfect habitat for the insect that drives Rom nuts: cockroaches.

Every evening, droves of them flew into the house, attracted to the lights. Rom and I danced like martial artists swatting them with broom, doormat, magazine, slippers ... anything we could lay our hands on. But we were outnumbered. The roof has to go, Rom declared. As layer after layer of tiles were removed, scorpions, centipedes, and ants came scurrying, slithering, and pouring out of their hiding places. Suddenly, one of the lads helping us yelled, 'Snake.'

It was a common sand boa. It must have climbed up a neem tree that touched the roof. That was exceptional behaviour for a burrowing species. 'If one sand boa can climb, why not another?' Rom wondered. But we haven't found another common sand boa scaling trees.

When Ashok Captain and Rom were writing the field guide to the snakes of India, they had long discussions about the name, Whitaker's sand boa. The name suggested it was mainly a terrestrial snake, but it preferred heights. Since it was a recently discovered species and people weren't used to the name yet, they voted to abbreviate the name to Whitaker's boa.

I hope that solved the signboard problem in Kerala.

Atomic Forest

If Rom hears a riff of rock music, he can tell you who played it, when, and the names of the band members. His memory includes musicals of the 1940s he had last heard as a little boy. His one big regret in life is his inability to play a musical instrument. He says if he had another lifetime, he would become a musician.

The love of music runs in his family. After six years in America, when Rom returned to Bombay in 1967, he found his kid brother, Neel, had dropped out of high school. Neel had taught himself to play the guitar and spent twelve

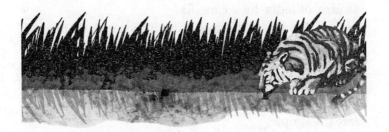

to fourteen hours a day practising. He really wanted an electric guitar, and, Rom, being the indulgent older brother, bought him one.

'It seemed like Neel's goal was to turn the entire apartment into an amp [amplifier],' Rom recalled. 'The music was loud and sometimes discordant.'

'How did the family tolerate it?' I asked.

'Everyone was supportive. Even Amma Doodles [Kamaladevi Chattopadhyaya]. She loved the Beatles and Rolling Stones, and she realized Neel was an aspiring artist. A film producer, Akhtar Hussain, and his family lived on the top and ground floors. Akhtar's son, Arif, was a singer who hung out with Neel. So that family didn't say anything. But other neighbours complained,' Rom replied.

Neel and Arif played in a band called Joint Collaboration. In 1971, they organized a rock concert in Bombay to raise funds for the World Wildlife Fund (WWF) with Granddaddy Harin playing master of ceremonies.

A year later, Neel formed a band called 100 Ton Chicken with bass guitarist, Keith Kanga. Later, rechristened Atomic Forest, the band performed at a tiny discotheque called Slip Disc, behind Radio Club in Bombay, and grew to have a devoted following. Neel was called 'the Jimi Hendrix of India' by the media.

I think Rom lived the musician's life vicariously through Neel. They may be half-brothers and separated by a ten-year age difference, but they are as tightly bonded to each other as identical twins.

Rom wrote lyrics for the band, but none was set to score. Here's a sample:

Hermits pound at gravestones on that road
Heads with minds oozing out everywhere
I hitched a ride on a careening time-toad
Salvation through a malevolent stare.
Back to a sliding aluminium station
You know that you've been here before
Climb off the toad and get congratulation
You've made it; you've been through the core.

Was it pretentious? Was I too boringly straight to understand this alternate universe of hallucinations? When Rom saw me leafing through the file of neatly type-written lyrics, he said, 'That's all nonsense.'

However, Neel was generous with his praise, 'They were really nice words. But at that time, we were not interested in doing melodies; we were more interested in jamming and playing our instruments.'

An album of vintage Atomic Forest—'Obsession 77'—was released in January 2011 by Los Angeles-based Now-Again Records. Since it's the only psychedelic rock album ever produced in India, it generated a buzz among music collectors. A terrible scratchy recording of Neel playing *Foxy Lady* at a friend's home provides a mere hint of his virtuoso. Have a listen on YouTube.

A reviewer at thestoolpigeon.co.uk says, 'I could name probably 100 current rock bands who would love to be able to reproduce Neel Chattopadhyaya's warm, fuzzed-up guitar sound.'

'Why the name Atomic Forest?' I asked Rom.

'Oh, I came up with the name. Obviously, there had to be something related to the jungle, and "atomic" seemed to capture the flavour of the time.'

Until then, I hadn't realized Rom had left a mark on India's rock music scene.

Nearly forty years after the lyrics were first written, Neel is now setting them to music. If Atomic Forest ever stages a comeback, Rom may have a music career in this lifetime.

Falling in Love

A few years after Rom and I got married, one of Rom's colleagues asked me when we had met. Without thinking, I replied, 'When I was fifteen.' She was shocked. She had jumped to the conclusion Rom and I had been seeing each other from the time I was fifteen. I didn't say anything for a few moments. Oh yes, I was evil, all right.

When my classmates and I were fifteen, we had to write our board exams, and we were under a lot of stress. We studied every waking minute: no television, no weekends, no 'wasting time'. I don't remember how I visited the Madras Crocodile Bank. Perhaps someone felt we needed a break and took us on an outing.

At that time, I had an infection near a fingernail. Instead of lancing it and relieving the pain, the doctor said the pus had to come to a head. Someone else advised my mother that sticking a whole lemon on it would quicken the process. So I wore a citrus on my finger when we visited Croc Bank. And there was Rom. I remember trying to hide my hand, but he remembers meeting a chit of a girl with a lemon on her finger. Our meeting wasn't romantic or even dramatic.

We may have even met earlier. Everyone who lived in Madras in the 1970s and 80s knew everyone else. It was a city in size, but a village by nature. Rom and my family shared mutual connections, such as Siddharth Buch, who was a prominent naturalist. My father went to school with Siddharth's sister and knew the siblings well. Rom also knew Siddharth, and there's a possibility we may have met when I was a child.

I graduated as a film editor and began my career editing soaps, advertisements, and corporate documentaries. It didn't take me long to get tired of it. Being a young woman in a man's world meant I wasn't taken seriously. Besides, the directors merely wanted an equipment operator, one who would cut a shot when instructed. I had hoped as I gained experience, I would be allowed more creative freedom.

In the meantime, Rom had made a children's feature film called *The Boy and the Crocodile*. To sell it to the European market, he wanted the two-hour-long movie edited down to an hour. Carrying an armload of videotapes, he strode into the studio where I worked. He claims we fell in love as we sat side by side, cheek to cheek, in the dimly lit editing room. I don't remember that. In fact, I don't even remember editing that film. However, I do remember editing his showreel, a short video portfolio of his work as a filmmaker.

He arrived one morning, dumped a huge pile of tapes on my desk, and said he'd be back after I finished the job.

Nobody had ever given me such freedom. When I was done, he picked up the tapes and vanished. He was going to the States to pitch documentary ideas to the heads of various television channels. I was just an editor, and he, a client.

At this time, I took a break from my editing career to apprentice with the foremost editor of the feature film industry in Kodambakkam. To my distress, he had only marginally more artistic freedom than I did. It appeared editors were merely technicians.

If I wanted greater control, I had to become a director. I was hunting for a suitable subject for a film, when a friend introduced me to a group working on snake conservation. They wanted an educational film to show at schools, and I was interested in the range of reactions people displayed towards snakes: from reverence to abhorrence.

Who do you meet when you want to do a film on snakes?

Rom said if I wanted to do a sociological study of people's reactions, I ought to meet Harry Miller, a Welsh journalist who lived in Madras. Soon afterwards, I got a big job: to edit a Hindi soap called Bible ki Kahaniyan ('Stories from the Bible') for Doordarshan. Career switch would have to wait. I had to earn a living after all.

The following months were hectic with high stress, little sleep, and many technological challenges. It was a nightmare to edit an episode, lay the music track and courier it to Delhi week after week. By the end of my contract, I was worn out and close to breaking down.

Meanwhile, Rom had a successful trip to the States. He had a contract from National Geographic Television to make a film about rats. Ana Lockwood, a common friend working on the film, invited me to Croc Bank for rest and recuperation.

Although I spent time with Ana, it was then that Rom and I got to know each other. Ana shuttled between the city and Croc Bank, and frequently, I had only Rom for company. He was fun: he cracked jokes, narrated his adventures, and took me snake-hunting. I thought when love happened, sparks flew. So when I fell for Rom, I didn't even know it. My holiday ended and I went back to the city refreshed.

I had an attractive offer from a new television channel. But I felt distracted, out of sorts, and disinterested. The walls of the editing studio crowded me, and the artificial lights made it seem like a prison cell. The mere sight of the editing console made me weary. My head was filled with thoughts of Croc Bank and Rom. All I wanted was an excuse to go back. Was it the open space of Croc Bank that beckoned, or was it Rom? There was only one way to find out.

There were no phones at Croc Bank in those days. Rom was surprised to see me, while my heart somersaulted when I saw him. I said I was going through a crisis and needed time out. He said I could stay as long as I wanted.

I hadn't noticed how blue Rom's eyes were. Or his long athletic legs. I appreciated how the golden hair on his arms glinted in the sunlight. And I was mesmerized by his dimples. The more I caught myself looking at him, the more I became certain. 'Woman, you are smitten,' I told myself. But was Rom?

He gave no indication he was attracted to me. I engineered romantic situations every evening: 'Rom, come and see, the sea is glowing.' We sat on the beach and watched the bioluminescent waves until dinner time. Or I would drag him out to see the crocodiles. Or some flower in bloom. 'Maybe tonight he'll say something,' I hoped.

By this time, Rom was working on his next film project: *King Cobra*. I made suggestions on his draft script, and he asked me if I would work with him. I didn't think for more than a second before accepting. Although I was excited to shift from editing soaps to producing wildlife documentaries, I was really waiting for another proposition.

He claimed he had been sending me signals all the time, but I wasn't reading them. Had I known his feelings, I would have made a move. Later, he admitted he was torn. Was he too old for me? Was it the right thing to do? How would my parents feel? With these preoccupations, his signals were so muted as to be invisible.

I wasn't aware of anyone else or any place else. I don't remember how much time passed until one evening, he finally proposed. I had waited for this moment, but when it came, I wasn't prepared for the depth of our emotions.

My life and career were never the same again.

Marriages are made on Earth

When Rom and I first became an item, many friends, his and mine, predicted our relationship was going to be short-lived. They made such a fuss about the twenty-seven-year age difference. It was as if I was marrying Methuselah. True, the age difference was greater than my age at that time. Instead, if they had said our different personalities and interests made us incompatible, I would have agreed.

Rom was a single-minded reptile freak who loved the wild and the company of wild animals more than people. I was a city girl. I had never been in a forest or seen a wild animal before I met Rom.

I chafed when trading colourful handloom saris for drab, jungle attire. I left behind armfuls of silver bangles, as they made too much noise in the forest. Beads could get caught in the undergrowth, so off they came. I confined my feet in shoes, a reminder of a hated school life. I didn't look like me anymore.

While camping, I became hysterical every night. I

thought wild animals were dangerous and out to get me at the first opportunity. To be zipped up in a sleeping bag inside a closed tent made me feel like chewing gum waiting to be stepped on. If an elephant came, how was I to make a quick exit? Rom tried to reassure me that elephants just don't do that. But I didn't trust him or the dreaded elephants.

I preferred camping near a village or staying at a hotel in town. However, Rom felt people were less trustworthy than wild animals. I nagged him so much he gave in on one occasion, and we camped on the edge of a village in Karnataka. Until late in the night, villagers watched us inquisitively, some flashed their torches inside the tent. They had never seen people like us camp in a tent before. Although their reaction was understandable, it irritated me nonetheless.

Early the following morning, they gathered around again, nudging each other, laughing, and staring. I learnt my lesson. Rom, to his credit, didn't say a word or display annoyance. By this time, I realized he was right: Elephants did not mess with tents. Perhaps they didn't know humans were asleep inside the flimsy triangular structure. It's amazing Rom put up with my total forest-naiveté.

The only source of nourishment at camp was instant noodles. I needed much more wholesome food to fuel the day-long and sometimes, late night hikes. But Rom lived on little food or sleep. When he needed a jolt of energy, he drained a tin of condensed milk. When we emerged from the forest, I ate unashamedly like a pig in village restaurants.

Speaking of those early days, Rom says, 'I was trying

not to chase you away. The first time I made tea for you, the leaves caught in your teeth. Remember?' I remember spitting them out with distaste. So the next time, he used a butterfly net to strain it.

'I knew I was throwing you off the deep end, so I tried to make things easier for you,' he continues. I was aware of the effort he was making, and that kept me going.

Despite our quiet attempts to reconcile our very different lifestyles, others only worried about the difference in ages. When I broke the news of our relationship to a friend, she protested, 'But he's so much older.'

'Yup, none of the brash, immature stuff. You ought to try an older man some time.'

'Think about it. You'll have to look after him at some point.'

'If we were both the same age and we grew old together, we'd be too decrepit to look after each other, no?'

She grew exasperated.

I was less flippant when trying to convince my folks. They too, thought the age difference was critical.

Even my father's cat seemed to drive home the age difference between us. The first time Rom came home, it jumped up on a half-wall behind his chair, and stared at its reflection on the little shiny, bald spot on the back of his head.

After much discussion of my unorthodox choice of spouse, my parents finally gave their blessing.

I heard snatches of gossip swirling around us. The conservative extended family sneered that I was marrying out of caste, religion, and race. Some made a big deal of Rom's meat-eating habits, taboo in my vegetarian family.

My parents had never given importance to any of this, so I couldn't have cared less.

Inquisitive strangers asked if I was Rom's daughter. At a college town, someone thought I was his granddaughter. 'I'm his wife,' I retorted, and they squirmed with embarrassment.

Rom and I set up Draco Films and began making wildlife documentaries. I wrote the script, Rom made the pitch, and we negotiated contracts and hired the crew. Initially, we worried we were making a mistake by working together. The highly charged atmosphere on shoots can create bonds or wreck them. Colleagues fell in love, had affairs, or fell out on location. Surprisingly, we enjoyed working with each other despite the pressure.

Two years after Rom and I became a couple, I met up with a few friends. One complained her husband was besotted with the latest electronic gadgets. I confessed mine had a weakness for the doll-like women from the Northeast.

'If these women visit the Crocodile Bank, he's out of the office immediately,' I said.

'You let him do that?' one asked.

'What should I do? Cover his eyes?'

They shook their heads and clicked their tongues in disapproval. Husbands, apparently, had to have blinkers, like horses.

'What's the point of setting an impossible standard?' I asked. 'He's going to look anyway, only surreptitiously.'

'Then he'll want to touch,' another warned.

'Perhaps,' I said, 'But I could also be human.'

'My husband is not like that, paah,' said another, as she shrugged her shoulders.

I didn't tell them how Rom melts when Latina women say, 'turdles and thorthoises' (turtles and tortoises). Obviously, I didn't know how to tame my husband, nor did I want to.

My challenges didn't lie there. They lay in the choices I had to make straddling two worlds. I almost gave up a social life in the city: music concerts, theatre, and cinema. During the early days of our relationship, Rom attended concerts with me, but I could see he was bored. I didn't insist on his company, but I went to fewer events.

However, I made up for the loss by gaining a whole new exciting world. As I grew more comfortable with the forest, every trip became a honeymoon. I was fascinated by animal behaviour, and how people related to animals.

Before we knew it, we had been together seven years, and neither of us was itching to leave. On the contrary, we couldn't get enough of each other.

Someone asked me recently, what was the secret of our relationship's longevity, given all the differences between Rom and I? I guess the differences were superficial: age, personality, culture, race. He reads science fiction; I don't. I don't like Frank Zappa much, and Rom can listen to him over and over again. We don't agree on many issues and argue a lot. But none of it matters. Not even Rom's appreciation of exotic women. Perhaps the secrets are having a sense of humour and not taking oneself too seriously. Maybe it is not taking the other for granted. I don't know; I'm no expert.

The only thing that matters is: Rom makes me feel whole. It will be twenty-five years this year, and he still makes butterflies flutter in my stomach.

Out of India

One of the few songs I remember from my childhood is:

My mother said I never should
Play with the gypsies in the woods.
If I did, she would say
You naughty girl to disobey.

In the song, the mother threatens to disown the girl, while the father promises to hit her head with a teapot lid. But she runs off anyway.

As a child, I read books that portrayed gypsies as fortune tellers, bogey-men, and thieves. Far from being put off by these negative attributes, I was intrigued. I loved their freedom of movement, to simply break camp and move whenever the spirit urged them.

Never having set eyes on a real European gypsy, I imagined our Korava were those gypsies. The Korava women, called *Koratti* in Tamil, wear glittering earrings and beads, and colourful skirts, albeit in a different style from European gypsies. I yearned to dress like them, but their style was too flamboyant for the staid tastes of my family.

When I grew older, I sought to know more about the Roma, as the European gypsies are called. I wasn't surprised their suspected country of origin was India, but I was appalled by their history of slavery, forced evictions, forced sterilizations, and jail terms for minor infractions in every European country. The Nazis killed an estimated 2,20,000 to 15,00,000. As recently as 2009, France deported 10,000 Roma to Bulgaria and Romania, both countries with a history of discrimination against the ethnic minority.

The story of our nomadic tribes like the Korava and the Irula is no different. They were declared criminal by the British colonial government, confined to camps, jailed for minor offenses, and had their traditional nomadic life restricted by laws. They didn't conform to the British idea of civilization, which meant settled agriculture and hard work. The nomads were seen as lazy freeloaders who paid no taxes and didn't contribute to the nation's economy. Even Indian society looks down upon these people of no fixed address.

In the face of such hostility, the Korava flaunt their differentness. Although the men wear shirts and lungi like villagers, they wear their long hair coiled in a bun, stride with muzzleloader rifles slung over their shoulders, and speak in loud guttural voices. Nobody messes with them for fear of receiving an earful of strident, colourful invectives. As a young radical, I admired their style and moxie.

Although little is known of the Korava origins, according

to popular perception, they came from the general area of Gujarat, perhaps Rajasthan. Angus Fraser, the author of the book *The Gypsies*, says the Roma came most probably from Rajasthan. So, was I right; could the Korava and Roma be related, after all?

In December 2011, Isabel Mendizabal, from the Universitat Pompeu Fabra, Spain, and a team of European geneticists examined the DNA of thirteen Roma groups from across Europe. They say the Roma migrated out of India 1,500 years ago, and the Punjab was most likely their homeland. I hope someone conducts a similar study of Korava origins.

I first met members of the tribe in person when Rom introduced me to Manangatti and Bangarapilli. They were master trappers and hunters, with remarkable skill in mimicking creatures' calls. A few enterprising Korava sold sacks of large bandicoots as feed for crocodiles and lizards at the Madras Croc Bank. Although the nomads don't eat the one-kilogram-heavy rodents, they eat anything else that walks or flies: jackals, domestic cats, palm squirrels, monitor lizards, and birds of all kinds, even crows and vultures.

I didn't realize how much my worldview was influenced

by the tribal way of life until a couple of months ago. When I found palm squirrels devastating our kumquat crop, I threatened to roast and serve the pests with kumquat glaze for Christmas. Rom was startled at my suggestion. I argued defensively; it was a perfectly logical solution.

Rom exclaimed, 'You twisted Koratti!'

I preened at the compliment.

A Poop Puzzle

The scat was crammed with ant exoskeletons. We found it under a rocky overhang on top of a nearby hill. We assumed it was pangolin poop. No other mammal of that size eats ants exclusively, and according to mammal books, pangolins shelter in rocky places. But neither of us had seen their poop before.

For confirmation, we sent a photograph to biologist-friend, Madhusudan, of Nature Conservation Foundation, Mysore. He hadn't seen pangolin poop either.

The only live pangolin I've seen was in Parambikulam Wildlife Sanctuary, several years ago. It had an elongated narrow snout with a lengthy tongue that picked up ants with the efficiency of glue paper. The claws were long and curved, to tear into ant nests and termite mounds. Its body was covered with large scales, and hence it is also called scaly anteater. The tail grasped tree branches like a hand, a rarity among Old World mammals. When one of us moved suddenly, it rolled up into a ball. After some time, its little beady eyes peeked out to see if the coast was clear. It was a cute yet bizarre looking animal.

Rom maintains a disdainful public posture about mammals. He calls them stinky and filthy, unlike his clean reptiles. But the pangolin's scale-covered body was freaky enough that he appropriated it, calling it an 'honorary reptile'.

The pangolin lives underground most of the time. A lucky few see it when it walks ponderously from one ant nest to another at night. Many communities that eat pangolin meat claim it is tasty. Because of the anteater's secretive life, no one knows if it is rare or common.

In Sri Lanka, we were excited to see a pangolin in the fork of a tree one morning. It was a once-in-a-lifetime sight, we told each other. But it remained suspiciously still for a long time. We eventually discovered a leopard had killed and stashed it up there, to eat later. Same place, same time the following day, we found another dead pangolin. And then another on the third morning. Clearly, that particular cat was a pangolin specialist.

Back at the farm, the thought of a resident pangolin was exciting. But Madhusudan found an online photograph of Cape pangolin droppings from Africa. Although a related species, it looked so totally different from the scat we found that we began having doubts. Cape pangolin poop was round, smooth, and almost white. The ants in its diet were completely digested, and there wasn't a recognizable ant part in the dropping. The one we found was long, rough, and black. If it wasn't a pangolin, what else could it be?

Rom and I wondered if it was perhaps ratel scat. We hadn't seen that before either. In fact, we have never seen the animal.

When we first moved to our farm, one of our Irula colleagues showed us a recent excavation by a ratel. The animal is also called honey badger in some parts. Known to be feisty, a protective mother can even chase away lions. Visible in the wide open savannas of Africa, the species is rarely seen in India. With its don't-mess-with-me attitude and ability to eat anything, I wonder why we don't see more of it.

Since I couldn't find a ratel expert in India, I sought the advice of Colleen Begg, a South African researcher. She said she has never seen ratel scat full of ants before, and she didn't think they could digest so much formic acid, found in ants.

If it wasn't ratel, the only other candidate was the sloth bear, which isn't found in this area. Setting camera traps at the poop spot would solve the mystery. But even if we took turns climbing up and down the hill, setting up and retrieving the cameras, it was strenuous business. We abandoned the pursuit after two nights.

At this time, with all other possibilities ruled out, we have to assume it's pangolin poop.

Unless one of you knows better.

The House on the Cliff

Rom seemed lost; he couldn't tell me where the old cottage had been. After all, more than forty years had passed and the entire area had been graded. Despite the presence of two hulking dilapidated mansions, I tried to imagine how the place must have looked when Rom lived here.

He remembered the house stood on a cliff that jutted out into Vasai Creek, with Borivali National Park behind and Nagla forest across the water. The toilet was an old-style outhouse.

'No one was about, so you could sit there with the door open and watch dolphins in the river below,' he said. 'It was the best toilet view I've known.'

In 1968, soon after Rom returned from America, he had set up a venom business at this spot, a village called Gaimukh Bandar, on the Ghodbunder Road that connects Borivali in Bombay to Thane. Here, he milked venom from snakes and sold it to the Tata Memorial Cancer Institute for research.

Snakes seem to attract the superstitious. A 'healer' brought a woman who had become deaf during pregnancy. He said if the tail of a cobra were inserted in her ear, she would be cured. It had to be a normal, healthy cobra, not a snake charmers' specimen that usually had its fangs ripped out. The only person who could provide such a snake was Rom. Although sceptical, he got a cobra out and did as the quack instructed.

Just then, a truck came hurtling around the corner. The driver saw this bizarre scene taking place in the garden and lost control of his vehicle. When Rom heard a huge crash, he quickly put the snake away and rushed to the accident site. Unfortunately, the truck had tumbled down the hillside, and the driver was grievously injured. Rom felt guilty, blaming himself for the accident. Thereafter, all quackery was held indoors, in the one room that was kitchen, lab, and bedroom.

Later that year, Rom moved to Madras.

When we visited Gaimukh in December 2012, I wanted to see the outhouse with a view. Sadly, no structure of that time remained.

'Who rented this place to you?' I asked Rom.

He couldn't remember. I called his brother, Neel. 'Bal Mundkur,' he answered.

'What!' I didn't doubt Neel; I was astounded.

'We met Bal last year and he reminded me he had rented the Gaimukh Bandar place to my brother,' Neel said.

A strange coincidence that had occurred in 1999 became even more bizarre. Rom and I were at the Chennai airport waiting to catch a flight to Goa. At the gate, an elderly man seated a few rows away looked familiar. Rom said he was a total stranger to him. I was so sure I knew him that I did something totally unlike me. I went up to the man, introduced myself, and asked if we had met before.

'Sorry, I don't know you at all,' he answered brusquely. Disappointed and puzzled, I returned to my seat.

When we boarded the flight, I found myself seated next to the man whose name I still didn't know. I introduced Rom and the man's face lit up.

'Hey, Rom. Remember me?' he asked. 'I'm Bal Mundkur.' I gathered from their ensuing conversation that Bal was a friend of Rom's family, and he had retired to live in Goa. While the two men chatted about the old Bombay days, I was struck by the irony of the situation. But I was also puzzled. I didn't recognize the man's name, and it seemed unlikely I had ever met him. Why then did he look familiar?

When we parted at Panjim airport, we agreed to visit each other, but we never did.

Bal Mundkur died in January 2012. It was only on reading his obituary did I realize he was a legend in the advertising world. Was that why he looked familiar?

I'm still puzzled.

To Culture an Oyster-catcher

I wanted evidence of culture in animals. Long-time friend and sea turtle biologist, Jack Frazier, suggested I look into oystercatchers. I expected a simple tale of each generation of chicks learning a specific behaviour from its parents.

Eurasian oystercatchers are one of the many wading birds found along the coast of India, northern Africa, the Far East, and Europe. They don't exclusively eat oysters, as their name suggests, but a wide variety of prey from worms and crabs to cockles. The ones that interest me feed on hard-shelled bivalves such as mussels, oysters, and clams.

When molluscs are disturbed, they clamp shut. The more I've tried to pry them apart, the tighter the shells stuck together. Despite having primate hands and opposable thumbs, if I'm defeated by these stubborn molluscs, how do birds with nothing more than sharp beaks for tools deal with them?

One group of oystercatchers specializes in stabbing

their prey in shallow water. To feed, bivalves have to open their shells underwater. The birds deftly plunge their bills between the shells, and sever the adductor muscle that holds them together. Once the mussels are immobilized, shucking them is relatively easy.

Another group of oystercatchers pries shellfish from rocks exposed by the tide, and batters a hole through the tightly closed shells. Within this specialty, some pound only the anal side, and others, the gill side.

Eating bivalves is a seasonal activity restricted to winters. In summer, oystercatchers poke around in the wet soil for soft-bodied delicacies.

Chicks learn one technique of opening hard-shelled molluscs from their parents and become proficient with experience. When they grow older, they teach their own chicks the same method. We know much of this remarkable behaviour from a paper written in 1967 by Michael Norton-Griffiths, University of Oxford, UK.

He swapped the eggs of stabbers and hammerers, and concluded the chicks learn the technique of their foster parents, not biological parents. It was a straightforward case of behaviour transmitted from generation to generation.

If learning one technique takes years of experience, could these birds change techniques later in life? A stabber which suddenly takes up hammering could damage its beak, and the bird might not be able to hunt until the bill grows out. Besides, Martijn van de Pol of Australian National University says, an experienced hammerer picks molluscs with shells thin enough to break open without risking beak damage; a beginner may lack this skill.

Stabbing also requires expertise. A mussel can clamp shut

around the beak of an inexperienced bird. Since stabbers hunt mussels wedged underground below the waterline, a bird trapped by its prey could be in serious trouble.

On his blog *Tetrapod Zoology*, British paleontologist Darren Naish republished a photograph of an American oystercatcher, a related species, whose beak had been trapped by a clam buried underground in South Carolina, in 1939. The bird drowned when the tide came in.

I'm puzzled there are no recent photographs or reports of inept chicks. If stabbing carries such a high risk, how do babies learn to stab proficiently?

'Young oystercatchers stab only small mussels, and there is little risk of getting trapped,' Van de Pol explains. This was the first of the contradictions that plagued me.

Since these birds are such finicky specialists in opening bivalves, I wondered how do they choose their mates? Would a hammerer pair only with a fellow shell-pounder?

'I never observed a mixed pair of adults,' Norton-Griffiths says. 'They always had the same specialisation, both food and technique. Which would suggest that they find mates out on the feeding grounds.'

But Van de Pol of Australian National University disagrees. He says in The Netherlands, the birds choose mates with dissimilar specializations, so females don't compete with males for food.

Could the English and Dutch populations have different cultures? Were the English more conservative in their choice of mates? Perhaps.

If a Dutch hammerer started a family with a stabber, would their chicks learn to hammer or stab?

Sarah Dit Durrell of Institute of Terrestrial Ecology, UK,

and her team showed most birds that probe for worms are females, most hammerers are males, while both genders stab. It stands to reason since females have slender bills, while males have shorter, thicker bills. If feeding technique were determined by sex, then obviously, males and females would have dissimilar specializations, as Van de Pol suggests.

However, did that mean the behaviour wasn't learnt, but came automatically, depending on the gender of the birds? Or do girl chicks know to follow mamma and the boys to learn from papa? 'We don't know yet,' Van de Pol replies.

There's more. What technique a bird uses is not dependent on its sex alone, but also its age. Adults eat hard-shelled molluscs, while chicks eat other prey like crabs and worms that don't require specialized skill. When one-year-old birds start eating bivalves, they stab. At two or three years of age, they learn to hammer.

Since a male oystercatcher would have likely spent a year stabbing before graduating to hammering, he ought to have little difficulty switching to stabbing should the need

arise. But a female may have a harder time hammering because her naturally slender bill is not made for a brawny technique.

Norton-Griffiths also suggested the birds' choice of technique is influenced by the nature of the substrate. If the soil is soft, hammering pushes the clam or mussel deeper into the mud; hammering requires hard surfaces. Then there are the qualities of the prey: if the shells are strong, firmly attached to the rock, and found in large clumps, oystercatchers don't hammer.

The birds would have to adapt to the situation to survive the winter, using whatever technique would provide access to the tender flesh of shellfish with least damage to their beaks. To possess knowledge of only one method of opening a bivalve would doom the birds.

John Goss-Custard and another British ornithologist, William Sutherland, refuted Norton-Griffiths' conclusion that oystercatchers strictly use one feeding technique. Although the birds prefer to use one technique predominantly, they also frequently use another method. Of ten captive birds they observed, two used all three techniques: stabbing, hammering the anal side, and hammering the gill side. If that is the case, surely the birds would have no problems switching foraging styles when the going got tough.

Are stabbing and hammering taught from one generation to another? The more I thought, the more they seemed to be innate behaviours.

After nine months of reading documents, writing to experts, and making little headway, I felt I was using the wrong technique: hammering at the problem seemed to sink it beyond redemption. I took another stab at the conundrum, going over every paper, verifying every fact, and finally, it became clear.

The 1967 paper offered no evidence of culture in oystercatchers. The main thrust of the paper was the role played by the substrate, the quality of shells, and mussel beds in the birds' choice of technique. Yet the author had inserted two paragraphs in the concluding section of the paper that claimed chicks learn a single technique from their parents that they use throughout their lives, and they teach the same method to their chicks in turn. Some biologists have repeated this myth from document to document, displaying behaviour they expected the birds to possess: cultural transmission of knowledge. And that was the source of confusion.

Four criteria determine how the birds open bivalves: age, sex, substrate, and the character of molluscs in the bed. Not culture.

While it was a relief to resolve the confusion, I was sad oystercatchers were no different from most other birds. But I remain respectful of their dexterity in dealing with hard-shelled molluscs.

Social Lives of Solitary Cats

Leopards are solitary animals. All cats are, except lions. The reclusive ones become social only when they court and have cubs. Occasionally, they may socialize around a kill. At all other times, these large cats are said to avoid each other. So it seemed incomprehensible that an adult male leopard in Akole, Ahmednagar district, Maharashtra, was babysitting a cub while its mother went hunting all night.

Vidya Athreya studies the ecology of these wild cats living in farmlands. She had trapped and collared the male leopard named Jai Maharashtra. The collar was loaded with gadgets to pinpoint the animal's location and programmed to text message the information every hour.

As soon as Jai was released, he walked six kilometres and sought shelter in a hilltop cave.

Three days later, three kilometres away from Jai's tryst with the research team, Vidya collared a leopardess, Lakshai. About twenty-four hours later, Lakshai left her sugarcane hideout and joined Jai in the cave. Were they consorts? How did Lakshai know where to find Jai? Was their meeting accidental?

Eventually, the two descended and resumed living in the farmlands of Akole. Although they met occasionally, they seemed to live independent, solitary lives. Perhaps their sojourn together in the hilltop was a coincidence.

Weeks later, Lakshai's GPS locations were confined to one sugarcane field for a few days; she wasn't moving at all. Vidya guessed she had a litter. At this time, Jai moved in with Lakshai, never leaving her side.

On a couple of nights, when Lakshai left the field, perhaps to hunt, Jai stayed put. It seemed as if he was babysitting while the mother was out. Accepted knowledge says male cats don't care for cubs.

Then Vidya received GPS information indicating Jai and Lakshai walked side by side along a path one night. On visiting the site, she discovered the pugmarks of two adults and a cub. Perhaps Jai was the cub's father, she surmised.

However, the result of DNA analysis was surprising: Jai was Lakshai's son. He was a few months away from setting out to establish his own territory. In the meantime, he was being a dutiful older son and protective brother.

Even tigers are proving to be family-oriented. Rajesh Kumar Gupta, the field director of Ranthambore Tiger Reserve, has observed two instances of adult tigers being affectionate fathers. He writes in *Stripes*, the bi-monthly publication of the National

Tiger Conservation Authority, that when the mothers and cubs met the dominant males, the little ones ran forward to greet their dads and nuzzled up to them like domestic cats.

In February 2011, a tigress in Ranthambore called T-5 died leaving two four-month-old cubs orphaned. It seemed unlikely the cubs would survive on their own, and the forest department began provisioning them with meat. The dominant tiger of the area, T-25 aka Zalim the Cruel, was an irascible fellow, chasing jeeps, and growling in annoyance at humans. It seemed likely Zalim would kill the cubs. Instead, to everyone's surprise, the adult tiger adopted the orphans. Although they were likely to be his daughters, such behaviour was unknown. Zalim taught them to hunt, took them on his patrols, and even guarded them against the unwelcome attentions of an adult tigress.

While the behaviour of Jai and Zalim may be surprising, tigresses and leopardesses hardly live lonely, reclusive lives. They inhabit a landscape of sisterhood: surrounded by sisters, mothers, cousins, and aunts. Daughters generally settle down adjacent to their mothers, while sons disperse far and wide.

We know adults communicate with each other through growls and scent marks. But in 2000, Elizabeth von Muggenthaler from the Fauna Communications Research Institute, North Carolina, showed tigers were capable of producing and hearing infrasound. Various uses of such low-frequency sounds have been suggested: to intimidate rivals, to paralyze prey, and attract mates.

Vidya suspects leopards may also use infrasound to communicate over long distances. That would explain how Lakshai knew where to find Jai.

A Cuckoo in the Nest

The pied cuckoo chick was a giant amongst its foster family of yellow-billed babblers. Every morning, for a few days, we watched the flock of dowdy, brown birds frantically stuff leftover dog food, insects, and other titbits from the garden into the gaping maw of the ever-hungry monster chick. The family must have been blind to think the fledgling with a pointed crest, prominent black and white plumage, and a long tail was its own.

Preventing a nest parasite like the pied cuckoo from laying eggs in its nest should be the first line of babbler defence. But babblers don't chase anything, let alone cuckoos.

Once a pied cuckoo lays its egg in a yellow-billed babbler's nest, the latter has no way of telling the difference. The cuckoo eggs, like the poor babbler's, are also turquoise blue.

However, pied cuckoos brazenly lay large, white eggs in the nests of red-vented bulbuls, whose eggs are speckled brown. The host birds are too small to dislodge the enormous cuckoos' eggs. Neither can they peck through the strong shells, among the strongest in the cuckoo family, and destroy them.

When a female pied cuckoo sneakily airdrops her egg in a bulbul's nest, the large egg crash-lands on the fragile bulbul eggs and often damages them. She might also deliberately push a bulbul egg over the edge so the tiny nest can accommodate her own.

Would bulbuls eject strangers' eggs if they were able to? Oliver Krüger, University of Bath, UK, conducted experiments with Cape bulbuls in South Africa, and found the birds don't eject any eggs, even small bulbul eggs painted white. Birds see colours better than we can, so why don't they shove the intruders' eggs out of their own nests? Perhaps it is not in their psyche. The bulbul can cut its losses by abandoning the infiltrated nest and making a fresh start elsewhere. But most don't.

Krüger found abandoning a nest comes at a great price. Predators are more likely to take chicks later in the breeding season and starting afresh runs the risk of losing the second brood entirely. Besides, there is no guarantee a nest will remain cuckoo-free.

Babblers may be cuckoo-blind, but why do bulbuls choose to feed these giant chicks? Early in the breeding season, the small birds chase away any adult cuckoos lurking near their nests. Yet, they don't seem to recognize the changelings that resemble their biological parents.

Pied cuckoos seem to have it made. But there's one trick babblers and bulbuls can learn to get ahead in this game of one-upmanship.

Nestlings of the superb fairywren of Australia look identical to those of its nest parasite, the Horsfield's bronze cuckoo. About four to five days before the eggs hatch, the mother calls to the developing embryos an average of sixteen times an hour. Each female embeds a specific signature code in her call that is unique to her and no other. When the chicks hatch, they include their mother's code in their begging calls, and the mother recognizes her offspring. No code, no food.

The incubation time of the bronze cuckoo is twelve days, three days less than the fairywren. Cuckoo chicks have less time to learn their foster mothers' secret code, and therefore, can't imitate it well. The mother fairywren doesn't recognize them as her chicks. So the cuckoo relies on other credulous hosts to rear its progeny.

Here in India, despite the gullibility of their foster parent species, pied cuckoos are not common. In all these years at the farm, we've seen babblers rear a cuckoo chick only once.

That's because the species of irresponsible parents haven't perfected one thing: timing. The cuckoos frequently lay their eggs late, and their chicks don't hatch by the time their nest mates do. The foster parents don't incubate the remaining eggs much longer and the cuckoo eggs rot. If cuckoos ever learn to time their egg-laying right, there's little to save their naive hosts.

The Name of the Snake

I was electrified on reading the newspaper that morning. Australian aborigines were not as isolated as we had believed. Apparently, ancient Indians had visited them. An interesting finding, but it had a major import on another subject.

Rom has long said the dog-faced water snake is known by the same name, bockadam, in Telugu and an Australian aborigine language. It seemed impossible that the name would date to the first migration of humans into Australia, more than 50,000 years ago. It also seemed too coincidental to expect two different races to come up with the same name independently. So how did the name come to be in two corners of the world? Since reading the news, I imagined a group of Telugu sailors either learning the name or teaching it to the Australian aborigines, 4,000 years ago.

The dog-faced water snake is found in lagoons, estuaries,

and mangroves from India to Australia. It's a grayish snake with some dark bars along the body. It is mildly venomous and not a threat to human life. In other words, there is nothing exceptional about the snake to feature in a conversation between two regular blokes of two races meeting after thousands of years.

But there was no mistaking it: Australian reptile enthusiasts refer to the dog-faced water snake as 'bockadam'. In recent years, the Australian population of the snake became a separate species and earned the name, Australian bockadam, while ours is called Asian bockadam or New Guinea bockadam.

Which of the hundreds of aboriginal groups used the name? Rom didn't know.

I sent out emails to reptile people in Andhra Pradesh, Australia, and the US, enquiring about the origin of bockadam.

Farida Tampal, a herpetologist based in Hyderabad, confirmed the Telugu name was *bokadan*.

'What does it mean?' I asked.

She didn't respond.

But Soham Mukherjee, another herpetologist, reported that Telugu snake hunters called the snake *neer katta paamu*. It means 'water snake'. As I suspected, the checkered keelback, the most numerous species of water snake, is also called neer katta paamu.

'I would doubt that aboriginal people had separate names for the different homalopsines [the family of water snakes to which bockadam belongs],' Rick Shine, University of Sydney, Australia, replied.

Come to think of it: why would Telugu people have a specific name for the species?

'I have not found anything that can help trace the origin of bockadam,' Harold Voris of the Field Museum of Natural History, Chicago, an expert on water snakes, replied. 'I can say that I doubt that its origin is from native Australians.'

'I actually believe the name has its origins in Indonesia, although some do say that it is an aboriginal name,' David Williams, University of Melbourne, Australia, said. 'I quickly searched some aboriginal lexicons but found no mention of it there.'

A few expressed ignorance, and others said they'd get back to me. Two months later, I had no leads.

Bockadam did not feature in a list of commonly used English words derived from aboriginal languages for Australian fauna.

I checked lists of snakes of every bockadam country in Southeast Asia, and they all used the name 'dog-faced water snake'.

There was little evidence of bockadam in any aboriginal language. Was it a pedigree Telugu name? I'm not fully certain.

I pored over Rom's snake books and discovered that Patrick Russell was the man who inducted the species into scientific literature in the late 18th century, and mentioned the Telugu name, 'bokadam'.

It seems likely the Australians picked up the name from

Russell's treatise *An Account of Indian Serpents Collected on the Coast of Coromandel*, published in 1796.

Although the Telugu-Aussie connection is not centuries old, still, the idea that a nondescript snake is called by the same unusual name in two distant locations, by two races, is appealing and intriguing.

Why do Men Rape?

In 2012, in the aftermath of the brutal gang rape of a young woman in Delhi that horrified the nation and the world, Amitabh Bachchan tweeted: 'even an animal would not behave so.' While he was referring to the brutality of the attack, some readers asked if animals raped each other. I answered: some do. Rape occurs across the animal world from scorpionflies and garter snakes to ducks, geese, bottlenose dolphins, and primates. And humans.

Lest some readers assume anything that's natural or occurs in nature gives it sanctity, or draw the conclusion that behaviour is hard-wired in our genes, I'd like to set the record straight. Animals kill their own babies, gore rivals to death, and routinely commit incest. Although humans have been known to do all that, as members of a 'civilized' society, we don't condone this behaviour.

But the difference between humans and animals is just a matter of degree.

Why do animals rape? Why did rape evolve at all? Unless we know what drives human behaviour, how do we deal with it? I'm limiting the definition of rape here to men forcibly committing a sexual act on women.

Among all creatures, we know of only a group of insects called scorpionflies that have a specific adaptation for rape. Males have an appendage called the notal clamp to pin females down. Even though they can rape, most male scorpionflies court females by offering a gift of food. But some discourteous males opt to use their clamps.

Ducks and geese are among the very few birds that rape. Most birds line up their cloacas, or orifices used for both excretion and reproduction, and males transfer sperm. But ducks and geese are unusual because they have an erectile penis.

Have penis, will rape?

There are often more drakes than ducks. When they pair off, a bunch of boy-ducks are left without mates. These guys gang up and jump on any duck that's isolated from the flock. So what came first in ducks? Penis or rape? Being water birds, drakes have to make sure their sperm isn't washed away. Could that be the reason the duck penis evolved? Or did it evolve to facilitate rape? I'll save that knotty question for another day.

Among mammals, rape generally seems to occur in species where males are larger than females. They use their bigger size and greater strength to have their way. Male chimps are known to be violent. But contrary to assumptions, forced sex is infrequent. Only 0.2 per cent of copulations observed in the wild are coerced, says primatologist Caroline Tutin. Perhaps male chimps are on their best behaviour because they cannot attain higher social status without the support of females.

Or, maybe the males bully the females so much that when the former solicit sex, the latter don't refuse. Whatever the case, female chimps avert copulation with males they don't like, say other primatologists.

Interestingly, bonobos, closely related to humans and chimps, show no signs of sexual assault. In fact, they don't display aggression of any sort. At territorial boundaries, where two rival troops would normally fight, bonobos have sex. Theirs is the most peaceful and explicitly sexual primate society known.

So our closest primate relatives, chimps and bonobos, are in a completely different league from us. According to behavioural ecologist Peter Kappeler and anthropologist Joan Silk, rape is 'regularly observed' in only two primates: orangutans and humans.

There are two kinds of adult orangutan males: large, dominant ones with well-developed cheek flanges, and smaller guys without the facial pads. All the big studs have to do is stay put in their territories and howl loudly, and the females zero in on them. They are veritable chick magnets. The smaller chaps have nothing going for them. Not only don't they have the physique, but they also don't have a territory to call their own. No orang female will give them the time of day. So instead of howling, these smaller chaps go prowling for sex.

Rape under these circumstances made perfect sense until biological anthropologist Cheryl Knott investigated further. She found female orangs sometimes resisted the flanged hunks and willingly mated with the unflanged males. What's going on here?

Not all large orangs are studs; some of them may be over the hill. While resisting such males, females may copulate with small males to save their babies.

In many primate societies, as soon as a male takes over a territory by ousting the dominant male, he goes on a baby-killing rampage. Bereaved mothers come into heat, and the new male sires his own offspring. Knott conjectures female orangs are somehow able to sense when small males are on the threshold of gaining dominance and mate with them. When they gain power, the new lords might spare the newborn if they thought it was theirs. But then infanticide is unknown among orangutans;, so what drives female orangs to mate with smaller males?

To add to the mystery, female orangs sometimes start out by protesting, but cooperate later in the same sexual encounter. Or, alternately, they appear to consent and then resist. Could these cases be called rape? Much remains to be studied and interpreted of orangutan mating strategy.

So why does rape occur in Homo sapiens?

Ever since evolutionary biologist Robert Trivers came up with the 'conflict of interest between sexes' theory in 1972, many theorists have cited it to explain rape. Since little energy is required to produce sperm, men can maximize the number of their offspring by inseminating as many women as possible. Women, however, are pregnant for nine months and produce one baby at a time, generally. Babies are born helpless, and mothers spend a considerable amount of time providing care. Naturally, women are fussy about finding the right mate rather than indiscriminately sleeping with many men. According to

Trivers' theory, this irreconcilable conflict between men seeking quantity and women wanting quality apparently leads to rape.

If this conflict is such a big deal, you would think human society would be polygynous: men taking multiple wives. Would such a society be less rape-prone? But what led many human societies across the world towards monogamy? It is practised in modern industrialized societies, sedentary farming communities, and amongst nomadic hunter-gatherers. The very fact most of us opt for a single spouse at a time indicates there's something else going on here.

According to cultural anthropologist Joseph Henrich, when a few men take many wives, other men are deprived of mates, similar to ducks. The intense competition between men for the remaining women undermines society, resulting in more murder, rape, violence, kidnapping, and poverty.

Counter-intuitively, our societies opted for monogamy, with some clandestine affairs on the side, to minimize rape as well as other crimes. Monogamy is a rare phenomenon; only about 5 per cent of mammals are monogamous. And still, we are grappling with rape.

Until the 1970s, biologists argued that men raped when they could get away with it, and their coercive tendencies were passed on to the next generation. Was rape a hereditary behaviour, then?

In 1975, feminist Susan Brownmiller came up with a radically different perspective. She said rape is used by '*all men* [to] keep *all women* in a state of fear' [emphasis in original]. Taking their cue from there, psychologists and feminists have argued that rape was a display of male power and dominance over women. According to them, rape was a learnt behaviour.

In their 2001 book, *A Natural History of Rape*, biologist Randy Thornhill and cultural anthropologist Craig Palmer suggested men rape when they don't have status or resources to attract mates. That sounds like the mistaken belief that small-built male orangutans rape because females don't desire them. Rape is a male sexual strategy to get around a shortage. It is inborn or innate behaviour. Dismissing the feminist argument, the authors declared rape isn't about power at all, but sex.

Criticizing the book, evolutionary biologist Jerry Coyne says it is 'the worst efflorescence of evolutionary psychology that I have ever seen.' Rape is pathological, not natural, he says. Are all rapists mentally ill? While there are many instances of sadistic rape when the rapist is turned on by his victim's pain and suffering, like the gruesome one that occurred in Delhi, the vast majority of rape cases are committed by seemingly normal men. For instance, studies in the US, for lack of any from India, show no pathological differences between rapists and non-rapists. Besides, rape is too commonplace to be committed by a lunatic fringe alone.

Studies conducted in Canada and US show rapists are more sexually experienced than other men. The assumption that the main culprits were men who stood little chance of getting sex proved to be incorrect. This blows a hole through Thornhill and Palmer's hypothesis that it's all about sexual access.

In the polarized atmosphere after Thornhill and Palmer's book was published, biologists heaped scorn on evolutionary psychologists, and social scientists seemed allergic to the idea that rape had an evolutionary history. Each side was keen to promote one cause over the other. Was rape about sex or power? Was it learnt or innate behaviour?

If rape was innate behaviour, it should occur in all human societies. But anthropologist Peggy Sanday found rape is rare in forty-five societies out of ninety-five, about which she had information. Rape is common in only seventeen; it is reported in thirty-three other societies, but there were no further details. According to ethnologist Verrier Elwin, rape is non-existent among the *Gond* tribe from central India. Anthropologist Jill Nash reports that the *Nagovisi* from the island of Bougainville, near Papua New Guinea, couldn't even imagine how to rape.

What explains the lack of rape in cultures such as the Nagovisi and Gond? How do these men manage to curb their sexual appetites?

The common patterns among these cultures are: minimum violence in settling conflicts not only within the tribe but between tribes, not glorifying masculinity, and holding women in high esteem.

But there are examples of tribes that use violence, but don't rape. The *Iroquois* was a confederacy of warrior tribes that expanded its territory by conquering others. When Europeans first arrived in North America, they were puzzled by the Iroquois' respectful attitude to women, even those taken as prisoners. The Europeans concluded since these Native Americans didn't rape, they must have a low sex drive.

Was the severity of punishment that these societies impose on a rapist a deterrent?

Among the *Minangkabau* in Indonesia, Peggy Sanday says a rapist's masculinity is ridiculed, and he may be exiled or even put to death.

The *Mescalero Apache* of Southwestern United States view rape as a cowardly act, says anthropologist Claire Farrer. A man who commits rape suffers a loss of face and does not even deserve to be called a human being.

It is extremely difficult to compare rape statistics and law enforcement across countries, because each nation defines rape differently. In many countries, rape is under-reported. But, there are numerous records of men raping when there is a breakdown of law and order, during wars and riots, because they can get away with it. The question remains: why do they do it at all?

Evolutionary biology thinks along two time scales: the immediate and the long-term. It's possible the ultimate motivation for rape is sex and reproduction, the biological imperative, while the immediate cause could be the domination of women, the sociological imperative. These two ideologies are not mutually exclusive as it has been made out to be. Different kinds of rape would have varying degrees of interplay between sex and power.

There are many ways to dominate others, but sex is used precisely because it is the thing being controlled. In sons-inherit-wealth societies, fathers want to be certain of paternity. So they use threats and violence, family honour, and chastity to control women's sexual behaviour.

How do such societies ensure women fall in line? By dangling the threat of rape. Men become self-appointed upholders of morals who can do no wrong, and women are like wayward cattle who have to be corralled, fenced, and watched over. Many rules govern women's lives, and the punishment for independence is rape. Some non-human primates control female sexuality, too, but comparatively, men in these repressive societies are extreme control freaks. And such societies usually blame the victim for the crime: she was dressed provocatively; she was drinking; she was out at night; she was asking for it... Sounds familiar?

Our close relatives, orangutans, differ from us in one fundamental way: the males don't injure females. Among ducks, several drakes may pile up on a hen in a frenzy of mating and drown her. Dolphins were in the news recently for saving a dog from drowning. But, male bottlenose dolphins are also known to form gangs that violently harass a female, sometimes killing her. It is hard to tell if these animals derive pleasure from causing harm, but it seems more likely these cases of drowning are accidents. So Amitabh Bachchan may be right; there's no conclusive evidence that animals, other than humans, are sadistic.

Men also control sexual access through physical assault, which male chimpanzees are suspected of doing. According to the last National Family Health Survey of 2009, 51 per cent of Indian men, and distressingly, 54 per cent women, thought wife-beating was justified under 'some circumstances'. Excuses for domestic violence not only include infidelity, but disrespect of in-laws, neglect of home and children, leaving the house without the husband's knowledge, arguing with the husband, and not cooking well. Societies with such sexist attitudes, according to educationists Laurie Bechhofer and psychologist Andrea Parrot, tolerate rape. Children of domestically violent households absorb the sexist attitudes of their parents, and the cycle is repeated in the next generation.

What is it about those particular environments that produce these terrible psyches?

Peggy Sanday explains rape occurs when men become the primary breadwinners of their families in cultures faced with food shortages. They have to compete with other men for diminishing resources, and violence becomes a way of proving their manhood. To such men who are struggling to gain control of their environment, women are no more than objects to be manipulated. 'Where men are in harmony with their environment, rape is usually absent,' she concludes.

Would warrior tribes such as the Iroquois and Apache, who raided rival tribal encampments, qualify as being in 'harmony with their environment'? While I don't know the answer, I find it intriguing that these tribes respect women as much as the matriarchal Islamic society of Minangkabau.

To sum up this complex story, biologically, men are geared to spread their seed around and can use their larger size and strength to advantage. If it were purely a function of biology, the 'I couldn't help myself' kind, rape ought to be more prevalent across cultures. But, instead, it appears to be more common in societies that denigrate women.

Biology merely provides men with the tools, but culture determines how they use them.

The Ironies of Fame

Rom's recognizability factor shoots up soon after one of his documentaries airs on television. Walking on the streets, we overhear loud whispers, '*Discovery*', '*National Geographic*'. At shops, restaurants, and airports, admirers seek autographs, take pictures, and ask questions. I usually pretend I don't know Rom on these occasions and skulk at some distance.

Recently, at a bookstore, a crowd formed around Rom. I looked up occasionally from a few aisles away to see if he was done. 'Is he famous?' another browser asked me.

'No,' I replied.

I was impatient to leave; the bookstore was one stop in a long list of errands. Besides, I figured if the man didn't recognize Rom, he wasn't missing anything.

But I must confess Rom's fame is useful on occasions. The ferry to Little Andaman had custom-built seats that didn't support the back, and the fixed headrest was too far forward. I squirmed, trying to find a restful position:

pushing myself far back into the seat, sitting cross-legged, propping my knees up, and padding my back with clothes. Nothing worked. I was resigned to another five hours of this torture.

Someone above heard my silent plea. A crewman brought Rom an invitation from the chief officer to the bridge. I tagged along, just to escape the uncomfortable seat. Rom did all the work: answering questions and posing for pictures, while I got all the perks. I read a book for the next five hours in a comfortable chair, enjoying the cool breeze and sparkling blue seas.

Sometimes, however, these instances of recognition go off the tracks. Rom can never be sure if people really recognize him.

We were in a bus full of holidaymakers going up into the hills of South India. I noticed a group of young people looking at Rom and whispering among themselves. The bus revved up the steep slope, and as it turned around hairpin bends, we slid across our seats. Despite being unsteady on his feet, one man from the group came up and asked Rom, 'Are you Ian Botham?'

'Who?' Rom asked.

The man repeated his question.

'No.'

The young man turned away disappointed. I laughed as much at Rom's look of puzzlement as the young man's question. Although Rom has lived all his life in this cricket-crazy nation, he hadn't heard of Ian Botham.

After I explained who his look-alike was, I said, 'You should have answered "Yes" just for the fun of it.'

If Rom has a gripe about his fame, it is this: all his fans

are men. He'd be over the moon if young women gathered around him.

'Making documentaries on snakes and creepy-crawlies isn't the way to attract girls,' I suggested. 'Try mammals.'

Apparently, he listens to me sometimes. He did a film on leopards, the first film he's ever made on a large mammal.

It occurred to me belatedly that women aren't throwing themselves at men who work with tigers and leopards either. Maybe wildlife is just not a girl thing. Then what is? Horses. But that's a sore subject.

When Rom was a lad, he was thrown off one, and he refused to saddle up for many years, until one momentous day in Arizona.

The lady of the ranch had to repeatedly reassure Rom of her steed's good temper. Even then, he rode ten paces and said, 'That's great. Thank you very much,' and slipped off the saddle. That was the only time he has ever sat astride a horse since that fall half a century ago. So, I know an equine film is unlikely, even if it means passing up the opportunity of winning hordes of female fans.

Recently, at an airport, a group of teenage girls recognized Rom. They squealed as they pumped his hand and took pictures. Rom grinned from ear to ear, pleased as a cat with a tin of fish.

Just as they were leaving, one of the girls asked, 'Aren't you Jim Corbett?'

For King and Forest

She was the first king cobra I'd met.

It was August 1993. The female king cobra had arrived for a newly initiated breeding programme at the Madras Crocodile Bank. After Rom released her into the enclosure, the staff and I crowded around to catch a glimpse. She remained hidden in the dark recesses. This shy creature was the longest venomous species of snake in the world. Intrigued, I returned later in the evening, when no one was about.

She lay coiled at the back of the enclosure, but there were lines on the dirt. She had been investigating. She became aware of my presence and lifted her head from her coils. I didn't want to rudely shine my torchlight directly at her, so I bounced the beam off the ceiling. To my amazement, she tilted her head up and followed the path of the light. None of the other snakes I had seen so far had done that. I wondered if she thought the circle of light was the moon. Maybe not; she had spent many months in another zoo.

She was an adult female king cobra, but she looked vulnerable. As she gazed at the ceiling, the little opening at the tip of her snout seemed to say, 'Oh'. Perhaps the Danish zoologist Theodore Edward Cantor, who described the king cobra scientifically, was struck by the snake's ethereal beauty. He named it *Hamadryad*, Greek for 'nymph of the woods'. Finally, I shone the light on my face by way of an introduction. Her eyes followed the beam, but I couldn't be sure if she saw me.

Every evening, thereafter, I spent quiet, meditative moments gazing at her. The fact that she was venomous was no worry because she was safely behind glass. Eventually, she grew used to the new enclosure.

As the weather turned cooler, I'd find her in the adjoining outdoor enclosure, enjoying the last rays of the sun. If I were late and arrived after dark, she would be draped on a tree branch, asleep with her eyes open. I tried to get inside her head and imagine how she saw the world. However, even after months of observation, she remained as unknowable as an extra-terrestrial.

My friends asked if it was possible to bond with a snake. I was certainly attached to her, but my feelings were in a different league from my affection for dogs. I was sympathetic, curious, and respectful of her, but I never felt the need to cuddle her, even if I could. It didn't bother me that she didn't reciprocate.

Other king cobras arrived, and they were just as gorgeous, large, and dangerous. But the first king cobra remained my favourite. Rom and the staff went to great lengths to simulate the conditions of a rainforest. During the hot summer, sprinklers wet down plants in the enclosures and raised humidity, while air-conditioner-cooled air blew into every king cobra's enclosure.

Soon after the king cobras settled in at the Croc Bank, Rom and I set out to do fieldwork. I disliked being in the rainforests of the Western Ghats. It was too dark and wet, and numerous leech bites dripped blood and grew itchy. We were travelling through the forests near Kalasa, Karnataka, when we received terrible news: the female king cobra was dead.

Everything I saw around me in the forest reminded me of her. The thick, springy leaf litter was alive with frogs and toads—prey of ratsnakes—which she would swallow like giant noodles. Cool water dripped down boulders and hillsides, and collected in pools where I imagined she would have loved to drink. The regularly spaced nodes of bamboo culms reminded me of the yellow bands on the king cobra's black body. By mourning her, I forgot my own discomforts.

Years later, the window that the nameless king cobra opened to her world remains ajar.

Driving while Woman

Rom drove the entire way on our first field trip. So I decided to learn to drive.

In a vacant lot, early one morning, Rom showed me the basics on his old, rattling jeep. I put the vehicle in gear and gave the accelerator a gentle nudge. It stalled. I turned the ignition again.

'Push the accelerator harder,' Rom exclaimed.

The jeep took off like a rocket.

'Brake, brake!' he yelled.

My foot responded by pushing even harder.

'The other pedal,' he shouted. 'The other pedal.'

It took a long moment, but my foot eventually obeyed. The jeep came to a shuddering stop a metre away from a lone palmyra tree. Rom looked whiter than usual.

When my pulse slowed, I asked, 'Shall I turn around?'

'I'll do it,' said Rom in a hoarse, low voice.

That was the end of my lesson. We drove back to the

Croc Bank in silence. Learning to drive from Rom wasn't going to work.

I enrolled at a driving institute and learnt to drive, even with cows, dogs, and humans unpredictably dashing across the road. Yet, Rom pretends he taught me driving. He tells anyone who cares to listen, 'Teaching her to drive turned my hair white.' Except, Rom's 'white' hair was a pale blond when he was born.

Whenever I took the jeep out, Rom mock-moaned, 'What have I unleashed on the world? Which tree are you going to find today?'

His jeep was a clunker. I almost wrenched my shoulder changing gears. The four-wheel drive mechanism compromised the turning ratio, and there was no power steering. Parking in busy areas was a challenge.

As if I didn't have enough to handle, in those days, bus and lorry drivers took my driving as an affront to their fragile egos and tried to drive me off the road. Women drivers were scarce, and hardly any drove a jeep. So Rom darkened the vehicle's windows with sun-control film. Except at traffic lights, no one noticed me behind the wheel.

Rom is susceptible to road rage, and over the years, I've taken over as the *chauffeuse*. He enjoys sitting back, telling policemen at checkpoints that I'm his driver, and providing backseat driving advice.

Nearly two decades later, after I had driven hundreds of thousands of kilometres through forests, villages, and cities without a single mishap, the Supreme Court banned dark windows. As we stripped the sun-control film, I wondered uneasily if the Indian male reaction to women drivers had improved in the intervening decades.

On my first drive down our narrow village road with clear windows, a public bus pulled off the road to give way. I waved my gratitude and he honked in greeting. Since then, I'm on hailing terms with many bus drivers. When Rom drives, they show no such courtesy.

People waiting for buses or gossiping with friends along this road frequently sit on the tarmac. When they see me driving, they get off the road immediately. Like bus drivers, they make no concession towards Rom.

I think they are polite. But Rom teases me: 'That's the confidence they have in a woman driver.'

While delivering saplings to the other end of the farm, Rom sideswiped the jeep against a tree. Now when I drive, others see the dented door and exchange looks that seem to say, 'These women drivers.'

In the past twenty years, highways have become better, and speeds faster. Maybe men keep their eyes on the road. Or, perhaps, they have grown used to women drivers. Whatever the case, I haven't been harassed. But Rom's teasing hasn't let up.

The other day, I was driving through a commercial section of the city, when Rom read aloud from a signboard, 'Janaki Driving School. Here's a great idea for a business. You can set up a driving school and a hair salon. Your sales pitch can be: "Get your hair bleached the natural way. No chemicals used."'

Presenting the Wild

I auditioned to be a presenter for a wildlife television series a few years ago.

Jonathan Scott, the well-known presenter of *The Big Cat Diaries*, gave me a master class. At the end of the first day of trials, he advised, 'Don't look so serious. Smile.' 'Relax. Move your hands.' 'Show enthusiasm.' How do you talk animatedly to the unresponsive black hole of a lens?

'How does Rom do this?' I asked myself.

I've always been impressed with his ability to say something sensible when the camera focuses on him without warning. The large eye of the lens doesn't influence the way he handles snakes and crocs. He's always calm around animals, and that was one of the first lessons he taught me.

Many of our presenter friends have Dr Sensible and Mr Drama Queen personalities. They are nice people, devoted to animals, in real life. But in front of the camera, they transform into feverishly excited caricatures. They prance around, snapping snake-catching tongs at a hapless, cornered snake. When it strikes, their voices rise in pitch as they shout, 'That's a dangerous snake.' Obviously, shy snakes become jumpy and dangerous when bothered. But audiences lap up their histrionics.

Rom's career in front of the camera evolved over four decades. Television crews loved the exotic combination of a white guy working with venomous snakes and dangerous crocodiles in India. He made an effortless transition from short films to hosting hour-long shows. While he grew into the career, I was jumping off the deep end.

Before leaving for the audition, I asked Rom for advice. 'You are a natural. Just be yourself,' he replied.

Being myself wasn't working. I wondered dispiritedly if I had to ham it up and become a blathering drama queen.

As a filmmaker, I had spent almost a year in one forest for a film, getting to know its seasons, rhythms, and animals. Since becoming a writer, I haven't been able to spend more than a week on assignment at a wild spot. I wanted this job so I could be forest-bound for a few weeks, at least. But was I willing to pay the cost?

In his films, Rom walked, jumped, ran, and dove after reptiles. I was trapped between the steering wheel and the door of the jeep, forbidden to get out of the vehicle within the National Park. So when the camera looked at me, I had to create drama with words, gestures, and facial expressions.

The big challenge was conjuring up something intelligent to say when the camera pointed at me unexpectedly. Exclaiming 'Isn't it gorgeous!' is the lamest thing to say, and I'm guilty of that crime.

'The trick is never to let the camera pressurize you,' said Jonathan. 'You have to be in control of the situation.'

He gave me examples, and he made it seem so easy.

During downtime, I came up with lines for imaginary situations. I tried different ways of saying those lines to the camera and seeing the results on screen helped me crack part of the challenge.

Then I focused on my next problem: my hands. Having spent long hours over many years around king cobras and crocodiles that are sensitive to the slightest movement, I don't wave my hands about while talking. For the audition, when I consciously stressed my words with hand gestures, I felt like a caricature of a gesticulating Italian and fluffed my lines.

After many takes of one shot, I grumbled exasperatedly, 'I need to practise moving my hands.'

'Before you came up here, what did your husband advise?' Jonathan asked that evening.

'He said to be myself.'

'Husbands should never teach their wives to be presenters,' Jonathan said, with a wry smile. 'Just as they should never teach their wives to drive.'

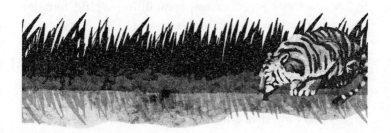

Battle of the Sexes

If females were freed of baby-rearing duties, would they turn promiscuous?

This question has been nagging me since I read evolutionary biologist Robert Trivers' theory. He says males get the maximum reproductive advantage with minimal investment, while females invest a great deal of energy and effort for a few offspring. This biological cost-benefit imbalance pushes females to be cautious in their choice of mates, while males philander.

What would happen if these sexual roles were switched? If males were left holding the babies, would they be faithful to one partner? Freed of responsibilities, would females become promiscuous and brawny?

Male seahorses incubate their young in belly pouches. I expected female seahorses to solicit sex from other males. But I was wrong. Males are apparently so eager to get pregnant, they compete with each other by snapping their heads at each other and wrestling with their tails while females coyly watch the outcome of these masculine brawls.

Although they can produce eggs within a matter of hours of meeting males, females play hard to get, demanding several days of courtship, says Heather Masonjones of University of Tampa, Florida. They deposit eggs in males' pouches where they are fertilized and incubated. Pregnant fathers pump oxygen, nutrition, and sea water for the growing embryos. Females do nothing further than check on their mates to whom they seem devoted. The unusual incubating arrangement doesn't seem to make any difference to sex roles.

If Trivers' theory is right, male seahorses ought to be choosy and play hard to get, and females would be promiscuous. Was Trivers wrong, then?

Masonjones measured the amount of oxygen the genders burn up, to calculate energy consumption. Despite all the hard work, males spend only half the energy that females do. Females exhausted from making one male pregnant aren't in a hurry to check out other males. Although seahorses swap incubation duties, they appeared to be monogamous: some through one breeding season; others for life.

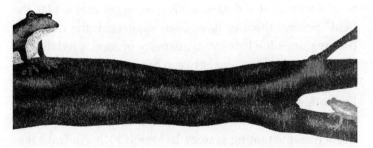

But pipefish, close relatives of seahorses, behaved differently. They share the same incubating arrangement as seahorses, yet female pipefish are promiscuous while males are choosy. Why did one fit into Trivers' theory so neatly, while the other behaved contrary to expectations? I looked more closely through scientific literature on seahorses.

Some are monogamous, while many others don't fall into any particular pattern. They live in groups, forge short-term and long-term relationships, and both males and females switch partners. Biologists continue to puzzle over other factors that may influence seahorses' sexual roles. So, I switched my attention to birds.

Sex role reversal is found in about 2 per cent of bird species. These are not weird or rare creatures, but common ones like buttonquails, emus, and some species of jacanas, plovers, and coucals.

Usually, male birds are prettier, sporting flamboyant tails, colours, and crests. But in sex-reversed species, females are generally larger and more attractive. They court males, lay eggs, and leave their mates to incubate them and rear babies, while they go off to find other males.

Why would males, who have it easy, give up their freedom to take on maternal duties, while freeing females to play the field? Several theories have been suggested: the nature of the creature's life history, availability of food, predation of offspring, and travelling between breeding sites.

In 2008, Hanna Kokko of University of Helsinki, Finland, and Michael Jennions of the Australian National University, came up with another theory: adult sex ratio influences the mating system. In March 2013, András Liker of the University of Sheffield, UK, and his colleagues, showed the theory had merit among a range of shorebirds.

If adult females outnumbered adult males in a species, then females were the child rearers. If males were numerous, they raised the young, while females gallivanted.

All this leads me to question whether caring and nurturing tendencies are innately feminine. They seem to be dictated by numbers, and by supply and demand.

Occupy Nest Box

A nondescript wooden box filled with odds and ends sat in a corner of the work shed.

'Perfect,' I said to myself.

I dumped the contents on a shelf and returned home with it triumphantly. Rom nodded his head in approval as I handed the empty box to him.

'I'll saw a hole at this end and nail the lid shut,' he said, as he dusted it with a rag.

I peeked into the plastic bucket to check on the three homeless owlet chicks. A dead palmyra tree that had been their home had crashed to the ground in a freak thunderstorm that April morning.

Once Rom completed the box makeover, I stuffed it with debris from the old nest and placed the chicks inside. I climbed up the neem tree at whose base the palmyra tree lay, and strapped the box to a branch.

I ran up and down the stairs throughout the day, peering through windows to see if the parents—spotted owlets—

had returned. They were nowhere in sight. I began to doubt if this enterprise of providing alternate housing for the chicks would be successful. Maybe the nest box should have been strapped upside down, so the hole was on top. Maybe the parents would be spooked, since the nest was even closer to the house than the tree had been. Maybe I ought to have fed the chicks before putting them in the box. It was too late to do anything but worry.

It was evening when I finally spied the diminutive parents preening themselves on a branch a foot away from the nest box. I ran downstairs with the happy tidings. But relief was short-lived. The following morning, the three chicks lay dead below the tree. The box had no baby gate. Had I strapped it upside down, the chicks would not have fallen off. I felt guilty and stupid.

Having lost one brood, the owlets were likely to nest again. But there were no other old trees with ready-made cavities nearby. So I turned the box upside down, and strapped it to the same spot.

The owlets adopted the box within days. Sometimes, I'd look out the window and be taken aback by a pair of large, yellow eyes glaring at me. A couple of weeks later, I heard

one of the parents call from the nearby banyan tree, and a chorus of chirps responded from the nest box. 'There are chicks, there are chicks,' I sang happily, guilt forgotten.

I looked in bird books to estimate the date of fledging. But in mid-May, a loud altercation erupted between the owlets and a pair of magpie-robins. The feisty intruders dive-bombed and harassed an owlet, while the chicks screamed from inside the box. The adult owlet fled. Later, I saw the magpie-robins dart in and out of the nest box. What had happened to the owlet babies? Magpie-robins aren't known to kill chicks, but the absolute silence from the nest box made my stomach feel hollow with dread.

I climbed the tree and peeked inside the box. It was empty: no eggs, eggshells, or chicks, dead or alive. Did I imagine the chicks calling? The only reasonable explanation I can offer is: the chirps were not made by chicks, but by mama owlet who may have been readying the box to lay her eggs.

Ownership of the box hasn't been resolved at the time of writing. At night, the owlets announce their possession of it, and at daybreak, the magpie-robins occupy it and sing melodiously in victory.

Meanwhile, I'm still looking for another box to put the stuff I emptied on the shelf. I don't know the antecedents of the dusty, old box. Until a few weeks ago, I hadn't noticed its existence, and now it is at the centre of a property dispute between two species.

Sensitive Predators

Crocodiles are armour-plated torpedoes. Their gnarly heads are all bone with no protruding ears or chubby cheeks. They are so strong that when one five-foot chap, whose mouth was safely shut with tape prior to being transported, slammed my ankle with his head, it felt like being hit with a heavy, wooden mallet. I was in excruciating pain, and hobbled for a week nursing a swollen and painful ankle.

Crocodile rivals bludgeon each other with their heads. They turn their heads away from each other, and whack sideways with force. There's nothing delicate about these head-banging brawls.

For years, at the Croc Bank, we knocked on crocs' snouts to make them back off. If large ones were intent on chasing us, especially when we were collecting eggs from nests, it took more than mere rapping to stop fiercely protective mother crocs in their tracks.

Then, in November 2012, I read a report by Duncan

Leitch and Kenneth Catania of Vanderbilt University, Tennessee, which said bone-plated croc heads were ten times more sensitive than our fingertips. My eyes widened in amazement.

Every scale of a croc's body is dotted with tiny pores. For decades, scientists questioned whether they were sensors for detecting changes in water pressure and salinity, underwater prey, magnetic fields, or electricity. Or did they serve a more prosaic function like secreting oils?

They were formerly called follicle pores, but now they have an impressive name: Integumentary Sense Organs; ISOs, for short.

Leitch and Catania discovered ISOs were supremely sensitive touch sensors. Just below these pores are quivering, raw nerve endings. A vast network of such nerves carries sensations from the face to the brain. To test the sensitivity of the ISOs, the neuroscientists used Von Frey filaments, fine hair-like nylon strands.

'We closed our eyes and tried to tickle each other with [the filaments] on our fingertips, and neither of us could even feel it,' Leitch said in an interview to *National Geographic News*. But crocs could feel it. 'My professor [Catania] and I didn't believe at first that they could be *that* reactive.'

Why do crocs need to be so responsive? When the animals are in the water, ISOs detect the direction of water

ripples caused by swimming prey even in total darkness. Additionally, ISOs inside crocs' mouths are also taste sensors, determining if that bobbing thing in the water was a rubber duck or a real one. Their most amazing purpose is sensing bite pressure.

A full-grown saltwater crocodile can slam its mouth shut with a bite force of 3,700 pounds per square inch, the most powerful in the animal kingdom. Come hatching time, those same jaws tenderly squeeze eggs to help babies emerge.

What prevents crocs from using their maximum bite force on an egg? For decades, Rom speculated every tooth socket must have pressure sensors. Now we know those pressure sensors are ISOs, densely packed around the teeth and inside the mouth. ISOs provide delicate sensitivity to crocs' bony toughness.

In the wake of these findings, the Croc Bank faces a challenge: How to control crocs with a soft, yet firm, hand? Rapping their sensitive snouts seems horrendous, and touching their chins is just as bad.

The staff tried rectangular shields of stiff netting, but crocs' teeth snagged on them. Lightweight plywood guards are set to be the next experiment, but it already looks unwieldy. Ideally, it would take a futuristic invention like force fields to deter crocs without touching them.

But how do crocs tolerate pain caused by head-bashing contests? Did the croc that whacked its ISO-rich snout against my ankle suffer more than I?

Or are crocs' heads like our palms that are capable of tenderly stroking a baby to sleep and delivering a stinging slap?

Unapologetically Child-free

When I was thirteen, I announced I wasn't ever going to have babies. I could tell from my mother's pained expression that I was being difficult. 'Why don't you wait till you're older before you make that decision?' she suggested.

Just a few days earlier, I had declared with the air of a haughty artist, 'Aesthetically, ears are ugly.' The only reason I remember moments like these are my poor mother's reactions.

Throughout my growing years, aunts handed me baby-cousins to look after during weddings and family gatherings. I was a girl and ought to have an automatic desire to care for babies. But I never felt maternal, no matter how hard I tried. I thought babies were like ears: ugly, alien, and unnecessary.

Most Indian families I know are besotted with marriage and children. As soon as I turned eighteen, the nagging began, 'When are you getting married?' Then I dropped

Rom, the bomb, on them, and after the initial shock wore off, relatives nagged, 'When are you having children?'

Nobody thought to ask if I wanted babies. I didn't desire them, nor was I convinced there was a good reason to have them. I imagined myself in my mother's position, and immediately baulked at the idea of bringing me up.

As an adult, I revelled in my newfound freedom. I had spent more than a decade dreaming of it. Having a child would put me under another kind of tyranny for at least eighteen long years, if I was lucky. And I would have to be a tyrant, too.

My friends, however, wasted no time in making the transition from brides to mothers. They sent euphoric emails with numerous pictures. I realized they were sharing their happiness; but still, their joy seemed disproportionate to the wrinkle-faced creatures they produced.

'What's the big deal?' I asked Rom with puzzlement. 'Anyone with ovaries can pop babies out, right?'

With a look of mock-horror, he signalled me to hush up before imaginary neighbours overheard the blasphemy.

But my attitude to baby animals was different. I watched Rom and the Croc Bank staff fret over the compatibility of reptile mates, the right conditions for courtship, and eagerly anticipate eggs and babies. Once they passed that gauntlet, they struggled to control humidity, temperature, fungal infections, mortality, and finding the right prey for the babies. If the babies survived past their first birthdays, there was a much-deserved celebration all around.

Many parents feel insulted that I skipped motherhood. One matriarch stared at Rom's crotch for several seconds, as if trying to divine the problem. Throughout the rest of our stay, she asked about which fertility treatments we had sought. I tried to explain it was a deliberate choice; I may as well have been speaking Martian because I made no sense to her.

As is typical on trains, after demanding to know what I did and if I was married, a stranger asked, 'How many issues [children]?'

'None.'

'Why not?'

'Because issues don't have fur.'

I went back to reading my book, while he spluttered on about how women are incomplete without babies. When I didn't rise to the bait, 'Who will look after you in your old age?' he demanded.

'And you have a pre-natal agreement with your children, right?' I shot back.

A few people wagered I would change my mind if a baby parachuted into my life.

'What if I don't?' I countered. 'Would you take the baby back?'

Now I was being rude, they concluded.

Many misinterpreted my words as criticism of their choice to have children. No matter how I couched my explanation, there was no way of treading softly. People saw my rejection of baby-dom as a religious challenge.

My child-freedom also poses another kind of challenge. For genes to survive, organisms have to reproduce. My poor genes watch helplessly as I happily, and without regret, consign them to a reproductive dead-end.

Ever seen a bumper sticker; 'We two; ours none'?

A Donkey of One's Own

Donkeys stood sleeping in the middle of the street, impervious to car honks and motorbikes weaving around them. It was our first visit to Chengalpattu town after moving to our farm. I remembered my childhood dream of having a donkey for a pet, while Rom remembered numerous stories of rabid donkeys biting people in Kenya.

'That's Kenya,' I retorted. 'There are no rabid donkeys here.'

'If they can get rabies in Kenya, so can the ones here,' replied Rom serenely.

And there things stood while we bought geese, chickens, and sheep for the farm.

Priya, a vet friend, invited me to go along on a home visit out of town. An exuberant pack of dogs greeted us, followed by a jack donkey. Yogi presented his large equine head for a scratch, and I fell in love with him.

I tried to photograph Priya at work, giving dogs their shots, but Yogi was attention-hungry. No amount of head and ear scratching was enough. When I ignored him, he snorted into the camera lens or turned around to display his rump. I changed angles and there he was, blocking my view again. I tried to shoo him away, but he wouldn't budge. I took pictures of him hoping he'd get bored, but he continued to pose. I didn't dare push him out of the way for fear of being kicked. He was as stubborn as a mule.

After finishing with the dogs, Priya gave Yogi a lump of jaggery. When he wanted more, she spread her fingers to show there was no more. He nuzzled her bag so Priya put it out of his reach. He casually and deliberately uprooted a houseplant and chomped it to bits. The household staff yelled at him, but unfazed, he looked at Priya to see if she had changed her mind. She had indeed brought only one lump of jaggery. He turned to destroy another plant when the staff chased him away. Yogi was unlike the over-worked and somnolent donkeys I had seen wandering the streets.

On my way home, I wondered if I was willing to pay the price of having an assertive and destructive pet donkey. I had collected and nurtured plants from around the world, and I couldn't imagine losing them.

Months later, Rom and I were up in Etawah, Uttar Pradesh. We stood in the shade of a lone tree on a busy road, waiting for others in our team to finish shopping. I watched a donkey ambling along by the side of the road, when it suddenly bit the thigh of a man pulling a heavy pushcart. The man yelled in surprise and pain. He had to pry the animal's mouth open to free himself, but it clamped its jaws on his hands. People came running from nearby shops and beat the donkey until it let go.

I stood rooted to the spot, too horrified to react. Rom advised the wounded and blood-stained man to go to a hospital for rabies shots, but the cart puller replied, 'Nothing will happen,' and walked away. Everyone went back to their jobs, and the donkey disappeared, too. The scene returned to normal so quickly that I began to doubt if the incident had occurred.

The prospect of a sweet, well-tempered donkey seemed to exist only in my head. Should I get a donkey? I couldn't decide.

In the meantime, we decided to get emus. At a farm, I was enthralled by the fearless, tall birds that lowered their hairy heads to look me in the eyes. We picked a pair of brown-striped chicks, when a filthy donkey with matted hair followed by a cute, chocolate-coloured, snub-nosed foal walked through the gate.

Reading my mind, Rom commented, 'Look at the mother if you want to know how the daughter will turn out.'

Passport to Andamans

The more Rom studied the map of Andaman and Nicobar archipelago, the more he wanted to visit this herpetological *terra incognita*. But his American citizenship stood in the way. In the 1970s, no foreigner was allowed to travel around this cluster of 500 islands.

Rom wanted to be a citizen of the Earth, but in the real world governed by laws of men, he had to belong to a country. With an American passport, he could travel the world with ease. If he opted for an Indian passport, he'd have to jump through onerous paper hoops to get a visa for any other country. But an Indian passport was the key to the Andaman and Nicobar islands. The decision was easy: he had hardly any money to afford foreign travel, and home was India anyway.

In 1975, when he surrendered his citizenship, an officer at the American consulate in Chennai put his hand on Rom's shoulder and asked him gravely, 'Are you sure, son?'

Rom was stateless for the year it took Indian authorities

to grant him citizenship. Far from feeling unfettered, he felt marooned on the mainland. He vented his frustration by collecting every book on the islands' history and natural wealth and learnt the name of every island. Never had anyone until then hankered so much to get to *Kalapaani*.

Soon after his naturalization papers came through, Rom set off. Ostensibly, he was surveying crocodiles, but he snorkelled in spectacular coral reefs, fished in the open sea, canoed up dense mangroves, and trekked through tall, evergreen rainforests, chronicling their unique flora and fauna. All wasn't well: crocodiles were hunted for skins, forests were converted to matchsticks and board, and beaches were mined of sand for the construction of buildings. But Rom was hooked. He would visit the islands a few times every year for the next three decades.

There was plenty of work to do in the islands—from coral reefs to canopy—and not enough researchers or conservationists. If the situation was to improve, more infrastructural support was needed. The answer was a field station with support staff.

Rom began raising funds to bring his vision to reality. He built a shack that was to serve as the centre of operations and researchers' accommodation on an acre of land near the present-day Marine National Park in Wandoor, South Andaman.

He bought a 40-foot trawler from Nagapattinam in southern Tamil Nadu, where the Customs auctioned fibreglass boats confiscated from Sri Lankan Tamil rebels. After the bullet holes were plugged, Rom christened it *Aka Bea*, in memory of a South Andamanese tribe that had gone extinct.

The next challenge was to get the craft to the Andamans. It was risky to sail the 1,200-kilometre stretch of open sea, especially when no one on the team was a professional seafarer or a boat mechanic. The Indian Navy came to the rescue and hauled the boat aboard one of its ships to the Andamans.

Alok Mallick became the base manager, and the rudimentary field station called the Andaman and Nicobar Islands Environmental Team was in business. Any researcher now had a place to stay and transport to get around. A small group of researchers began documenting species and studying the impact of development on the islands and its wild denizens. In the early 1990s, the station moved to its current five-acre spread, wedged between mangroves and rainforest.

Today, the base is a hive of research activity: drafting management recommendations on many aspects of island ecology, studying anthropology, and conducting surveys of plants, reptiles, and coral reefs. Two dugout canoes, ten wooden cottages built Burmese style, and a well-stocked library are utilized by numerous research and conservation organizations based on the mainland.

In the meantime, Indian authorities relaxed travel restrictions on foreigners visiting the Andamans, but the Nicobars remain out of bounds.

'Are you tempted to reclaim your American citizenship?' I asked Rom the other day.

'Are you kidding?'

Loss of a Colleague

We were newbie producers: Rom had done one wildlife documentary, and I had no experience at all. There was little chance of *National Geographic* Television commissioning us to do a film on king cobras.

In our naiveté, Rom and I wrote to the best wildlife filmmakers in the world, asking if they'd collaborate. Some said they were busy until their next lifetime, while others didn't bother to respond.

Fellow Indian filmmakers gently suggested we had a bomb. No matter what the snake's emotional state, it always had the same expressionless face. We'd never be able to sustain a 52-minute documentary, they said. In fact, no film had ever been made on one species of snake.

A film crew from Bristol, UK, arrived at the Croc Bank to shoot a sequence for a series called *Nightmares of Nature*. The producer-cameraman Richard Matthews had just made the spectacular *Crater of the Rain God*. Rom and I liked his relaxed manner, problem-solving skills, and his fantastic shots, and we wanted to work with him.

If Richard had any misgivings about our ambition, he didn't show it. *National Geographic* was happy with our collaboration and we got the commission. The first months of filming were rough. Richard was working on another film and sent a cameraman who normally filmed tiny creatures in small sets.

Every time we asked him, 'Did you get the shot?' He'd reply, 'Light was too low'; 'the snake was too far away'; 'the snake came too close to the lens'. We grew despondent, uncertain if we were getting any shots.

In those days, prior to high-definition video, we shot on film that was sent to Bristol for processing and transferring to videotapes. Usually, producers saw this raw footage called 'rushes' or 'dailies' the same day, but we could only see them after many weeks. We were working virtually blindfolded.

Then Richard arrived. Although he, too, operated a clunky film camera, he was much lighter on his feet. He didn't wait for the creature to crawl into focus; instead, he worked around the animal. We didn't have to ask if he got the shot. Not only did he get it, but he also had the action covered in various focal lengths, essential for an editor to create a story sequence. He made filming wildlife seem effortless.

The king cobra film won an Emmy for Outstanding News and Documentary Program Achievement in 1998. Neither Rom nor I knew what an Emmy was. Richard said it was big. When Rom heard he had to wear a tuxedo to the event at Marriott Marquis at Times Square, New York, he said, 'Bah! I'm not going.'

'It's the biggest thing in television,' Richard said, trying to change Rom's mind. But Rom was adamant and his golden statuette came in the mail.

We produced other films with Richard. On one shoot, an unreasonable cameraman was giving me hell. Richard commiserated saying he began his career in filmmaking as an associate producer, and he had such a bad time with an A-list cameraman that he decided to become a cameraman himself. His camera work was so good, I had mistakenly assumed he turned producer after gaining his spurs as a cameraman.

At the turn of the millennium, the bottom fell out of the wildlife documentary business. Commissions were harder to get, budgets shrank, and production values plummeted. I quit producing, while Richard decided this was the right time to move his young family to his native South Africa.

He began to specialize in aerial filming, testing gear, and building contraptions to get better shots. Rom and Richard continued to bat ideas back and forth for films and television series. But none materialized.

In the first week of March 2013, an email from Richard's former assistant brought tragic news. Richard didn't survive a plane crash in the Namibian desert.

Who knows what Rom's and my history as filmmakers might have been had Richard not taken a gamble.

Scapegoats on Eight Legs

The agony of the woman in the documentary film was palpable. She said the pain was unbearable and necrosis was eating her finger. Her finger had been amputated joint by joint as the rot spread. Other case histories followed; the culprit in every case was the same species of spider: the brown recluse of America. Modern medicine seemed to be helpless against this tiny two-centimetre-long creature.

I asked Dr David Warrell, an authority on treating venomous animal bites, about blaming the brown recluse for these horrors. He dismissed my concerns, saying I ought not to trust my fellow filmmakers. 'But what else could cause such horrific symptoms?' I persisted.

'It could be almost anything. These are unverified cases, and I wouldn't consider them spider bites without evidence.'

'Does he have to see the spider biting the person before he will call it a spider bite?' I grumbled to myself.

In a medical review, entomologist Richard Vetter

and toxinologist Geoffrey Isbister note several medical conditions mimic spider bite symptoms, including bacterial and viral infections, diseases, allergies, and flea and bed bug bites. In an American national study, about 30 per cent of patients with skin lesions claimed to have been bitten by spiders, when they actually suffered from an infection caused by methicillin-resistant *Staphylococcus aureus* (MRSA).

Spiders take the rap from both the uninformed and doctors. Florida's poison control centres received 844 reports of brown recluse bites over a six-year-period, 15 per cent from medical personnel. But only seventy recluse spiders have been found in Florida in 100 years. No wonder David was particular about evidence.

To confirm a case of spider bite, clinicians need all of these three criteria to be fulfilled: records of the clinical effects of the bite, the spider caught at the time of bite, and its identity determined by an expert.

Fifteen years ago, Phillip Anderson, a Missouri physician and recluse expert, said although several deaths caused by recluses have been reported, not one has been proven. That remains true today.

In reality, spiders are better behaved than we give them credit. In six months, one family in Kansas collected 2,055 recluse spiders from their home. In an Oklahoma barn,

spider-hunters caught 1,150 over three nights. Despite these high numbers, no human resident was bitten. They are, after all, called recluses for a reason.

What about India? Is any species dangerous to human life? In early May 2012, villagers in Sadiya, near the Assam-Arunachal Pradesh border, claimed swarms of spiders were attacking them. A man and a boy were purportedly killed in Tinsukia district. Some newspapers wildly claimed the creatures were black widow spiders. How did these natives of North America find their way to remote Assam?

Tarantula expert Manju Siliwal at Wildlife Information Liaison Development Society, Coimbatore, visited the area during the panic. No one witnessed a spider biting anyone. No autopsy of the two purported victims was done. The rumour began with a television reporter. Manju identified a specimen a villager had caught as *Chilobrachys assamensis*, a tarantula until then known from Sivasagar, almost 200 kilometres away.

I did find a spider bite victim closer to home: Mittal Gala, who used to work at the Croc Bank. She said the bite of a captive Indian ornamental tarantula from the Western Ghats caused extreme pain for about six hours and muscle cramps for a week. She couldn't hold a pen for more than five minutes or walk more than fifty steps. But the symptoms passed without permanent effects. That's the most serious case of a confirmed spider bite we've heard in India.

David and colleagues from Oxford, UK, reported hobbyists bitten by pet Indian ornamental tarantulas also suffered from local swelling, rash, and shivering, besides severe pain and muscle cramps.

Spiders are reticent to bite. Unfortunately, we are too quick to believe rumours of how terrible they are. There's no doubt a few spiders cause immense human misery worldwide, but should we indict the entire lot of them?

Hunting by Mimicry

Rom was astonished when the chicken-sized megapode responded to his field assistant, Theodorus. Both men were hiking through the forest near Muting, Irian Jaya, now called West Papua, when Theo picked up one of the numerous nuts from the forest floor. A borer had neatly incised a hole in the shell and hollowed out the oil-rich kernel.

Hidden behind palm fronds laced together, Theo pressed the nut to his lips and whistled, mimicking the call of a male megapode. Within minutes, a male answered. Theo continued to whistle until the bird came closer and closer. Once it was within sight, he felled it with an arrow. He had three megapodes lying dead inside the hide in half an hour.

Mimicking the bird is not as simple as blowing a hollow nut. When Rom tried Theo's trick, he sounded like a megapode burp.

Although expert mimicry of animal calls is an admired skill in humans, do animals mimic other animals to their own advantage?

Tribals in the Nilgris have long said tigers mimic their prey as a hunting strategy. During the British Raj, hunters noted tigers 'pook', a sound remarkably like the alarm call of sambhar. George Schaller describes in *The Deer and the Tiger*, 'It is a loud, clear "pok," somewhat flatter in tone and lacking the resonance of the deer call; it is given once or several times in succession.' Why do tigers mimic sambhar calls? Is it to lure them close enough to ambush?

Schaller combed through the writings of hunters and naturalists of the colonial era like F.W. Champion, A.A. Dunbar-Brander, and E.S. Lewis. Tigers seemed to mimic sambhar alarm call while peeing, approaching a kill, disturbed at a kill by man, leading a male tiger away from a kill, seeing a man on a tree, and when shot. In fact, tigers seem to pook on every occasion except hunting.

Yet, some thought pooking was a hunting strategy, while others thought it was a mating call. During the course of his two-year study, Schaller heard tigers pooking to each other, but none during a hunt. He surmised they advertise their presence to prevent sudden encounters. Perhaps the resemblance to sambhar alarm call is a mere coincidence.

The Nilgris' tribes aren't the only ones to believe in tigers' mimicking skills. According to hunters' lore in faraway Siberia, not only do Amur tigers imitate the calls of Asian black bears, a regular part of the cats' diet, but also bears' prey to attract bears. Could there be something more to tiger pooking?

Biologists of the Wildlife Conservation Society observed a troop of pied tamarins, squirrel-sized primates, feeding on a fig tree in the Brazilian Amazon, when they heard the distress call of a tamarin pup from a thicket of lianas. The leader of the monkey troop descended from the tree to investigate while urging the rest to flee. Ignoring his directions, three other monkeys followed him, concerned for the young one.

Suddenly, a margay, a spotted cat smaller than a house cat, leapt from the tangle of vegetation and walked towards the tamarin troop. The chief screamed and the troop fled. Although the trick didn't yield any tamarins that time, mimicking a young prey animal in distress is a cunning ploy. It's possible margays learn the behaviour from their mothers who teach them to hunt, so the trick may be shared by families.

Amerindians say other cats like cougars, ocelots, and jaguars also mimic a range of prey from rodents like agoutis to short, plump, flightless tinamous birds.

If margays can mimic their prey to fool them, is it possible tigers do the same? Interestingly, despite many enthusiasts and biologists observing tigers, we don't know yet.

Season of Leeches

The morose ranger rolled up his pant legs to reveal his secret protection: sheer black pantyhose. He feared leeches so much he even resorted to cross-dressing. I repressed a smile and remembered the horror of my first leech bite.

Rom and I had trekked all morning through a forest to reach the top of a spectacular waterfall. As I marvelled at the water crashing on the rocks below, I noticed a trickle of bright red blood between my toes. I unstrapped my walking sandals, and tried to pull off the slippery, blood-gorged, grape-like leech.

Watching my desperate attempts, Rom said, 'Let it be. It'll fall off on its own.' Let it be? It was drinking my blood, for crying out loud! I managed to get it off my leg, but it stuck to my hand. Getting rid of it wasn't easy. Like snot.

After I flicked it off, I watched with dismay as blood flowed freely from the wound—leech saliva has anti-coagulating enzymes—while Rom gushed on about the scenic beauty of the waterfall.

Forest villagers used their machetes to scrape leeches off their bare legs. Some applied snuff mixed with petroleum jelly, but most let the worms drink and drop. Researchers sprayed insecticide, but Rom worried that rains would wash these dangerous chemicals on to the forest floor.

'It's just a few drops of blood,' I consoled myself. 'I'm part of the food chain.'

I learnt to ignore leech bites and they healed in less than forty-eight hours. Occasionally, I scratched them in my sleep and woke up the following morning to the horror of white bed sheets stained with blood in the homes of friends and tea estate guest houses.

I read about workers in Malaysian rubber plantations using 'leech socks'. Leeches can wriggle through knitted socks but not through tightly woven cotton fabric.

Based on the description, my mother crafted large, green Christmas stockings that were fastened with a drawstring above the knee. In the early 1990s, Rom and I sashayed through the dark, dense forests of the Western Ghats in our baggy leggings, setting a fashion trend. Now leech socks have become standard-issue rainforest accessory.

Before heading out on one forest walk, a colleague and Rom insisted leeches weren't about, and there was no need to wear leech socks. Wouldn't you know it? Zillions of leeches advanced towards us, the worst outbreak I had ever seen in my life. The leaf litter seemed to be alive and in a ravenous hurry to reach us, their buffet.

The men dashed through the forest, hoping to outrun the bloodsuckers, but instead, they lost me. I had myself to blame. Kitted out in my leech socks, I was lagging behind.

Exhaustion and hunger brought macabre thoughts. If I

fell and broke my legs, how would I deal with the legions of leeches? Could they suck me dry? Such thoughts steadied my stumbling feet as I stepped over exposed roots.

An hour later, I was relieved when I found my way back. I expected the men to make amends for abandoning me. Instead, they were stripped down to their underwear, counting their leech bites. Rom grinned with pride when he won with a score of 132.

In reality, leeches are benign; they don't transmit diseases. Snakes may be the symbol of medicine in the West. But in Hinduism, Dhanvantri, the physician of the gods, is portrayed with a leech in one of his hands. But the slimy worms are reviled, perhaps more than any other creature.

People display unbelievable cruelty to leeches—snipping them in half with scissors, burning them with cigarette butts, and sprinkling salt or insecticide on them—and take satisfaction as the itsy-bitsy creatures writhe to death. Some folks then hold forth on how farmers and villagers should learn to live with large, dangerous animals and express strong opinions against holding dolphins in captivity.

If it weren't for leeches, I wouldn't know such anomalies as devoted wife-deserters, or conservation-minded torturers.

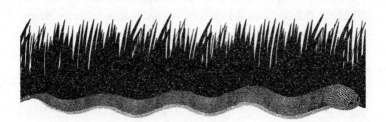

Luring Butterflies

A cloud of yellow butterflies swarms around Mauricio Babilonia's head in *One Hundred Years of Solitude*, one of the novel's deeply evocative images. The insects are so devoted to him that they herald his arrival to his lover, Meme. Initially, I thought if this character has his own host of ethereal beauties reminiscent of fragrant flowers and sweet nectar, he must be special.

When we moved to our farm, we let wild grasses and weeds blanket the ground. After rains, a multitude of yellow, white, and orange butterflies flitted in the sun. When I set up a garden, I paid the price for having these beautiful creatures. Voracious caterpillars advanced like blight. I concocted all kinds of herbal juices to deter them, but my spells didn't work.

We planted trees that shaded out the grass and weeds, and those butterflies were replaced by larger ones like crimson rose, common crow, and blue tiger. They swarmed around the flowers of one tree in particular: the divi-divi.

The flowers of the attractive native of the Caribbean have a heady fragrance, and butterflies hang from them in clusters, like fruit. By this time, I had abandoned gardening altogether and gave the caterpillars a free run of the garden. Now, when large blue Mormons flash their startling bluish-white wings, our eyes glaze over from wonderment.

Years after I read Gabriel Garcia Márquez's tale, I had my own Mauricio moment. Rom and I were following a dry streambed through a rainforest on a hot, sunny morning. A bevy of common bluebottle butterflies and other assorted species hovered around me, resting on my head and shoulders when I paused to catch my breath. Some settled along the length of my bare arms. Even though cicadas sang loud enough to drown any other sound, I could hear the paper-like wings beating above my head. Some butterflies were so anxious to get close, they brushed softly against my face. I didn't want to leave the moving halo behind, even though a steaming hot meal awaited us at camp.

Our visit coincided with the first monsoon that triggered the simultaneous hatching of many species of butterflies from their chrysalises. Smelly sweat seems to attract butterflies more than sweet-smelling flowers. In the tropical humidity, my clothes were soaked and my skin was covered in salty sweat. I was just a butterfly feeder on the move, not the Chosen One.

In *One Hundred Years of Solitude*, the butterflies don't leave Mauricio alone. Fluttering about in a scorpion-overrun bathroom where he makes love to Meme, they give away his presence. An armed sentry posted by Fernanda,

Meme's mother, shoots Mauricio, paralyzing him. Instead of representing all things sunny, sweet and colourful, in the book, a host of these ethereal creatures is a harbinger of tragedy.

For one of our films, Rom and I wanted to do a butterfly sequence. No matter how much I stank, I couldn't attract clouds of them. To go looking for butterflies would be like chasing will-o'-the-wisps. One knowledgeable friend suggested baiting butterflies with overripe fruit. We split open a jackfruit that was on the verge of fermenting and placed it in a clearing and waited. Nothing happened.

Someone else suggested we pour rum on the fruit. Hours passed and the fruit stank. But no butterflies came. By mid-afternoon, with few daylight hours left, we began to get desperate. Another suggested urinating on the fruit. Even that failed to lure the insects. At sunset, we gave up and turned our attention to other shots.

The following afternoon, one of the trackers said butterflies were swarming on the fruit. We ran down to the clearing and found moths, butterflies, and flies jostling for space on the fermenting, fetid fruit.

Here's my question to Márquez: to have all those butterflies flutter about Mauricio, how did he smell?

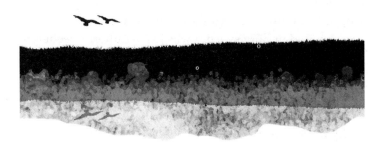

Spotting the Killer

A leopard was shot dead in Mandi district, Himachal Pradesh, on 11 August 2013, on the charge of man-eating. Newspaper reports say its stomach had the remains of a dog, not a human.

Conservationists were outraged that an innocent leopard had been killed. Between the last human death on July 28 and the leopard's death, two full weeks passed, as would have any human flesh in the gut. How was a hunter to divine if the animal in his sights was a man-eater?

Two nights later, another person was attacked. Perhaps an innocent animal had indeed been destroyed. Or perhaps there was more than one man-eater.

Understandably, villagers wanted the area rid of the man-eater. But what does the animal look like, and how does one identify it?

Leopards do not live in exclusive zones. A male's territory may overlap with that of a couple of females. A mother leopardess may have grown cubs living with her. How does one deduce which animal was the culprit?

Rom and I visited Lakhpat Singh Rawat, a licensed man-eater slayer, in the neighbouring state of Uttarakhand, in December 2012. In mid-November, a leopard had taken a five-year-old boy at Gauchar.

Although Rawat combed the area every evening, the trail was cold. The scratches on a nearby tree, where a leopard had raked its claws, were the only evidence of the cat's presence.

Rawat is a school teacher who took up the gun in the year 2000 after he lost twelve students to leopards. In an email, he had said he studies the pugmarks of the man-eater at the site of the tragedy and tracks the animal's movements for up to twenty-five days. Only when he's certain it's a man-eater, does he take a shot. We weren't convinced. The tracks of average adult leopards look identical, and this method has been scientifically discredited.

Rawat then said when his spotlight picked up the reflective eyes of a leopard, he had only three seconds to decide if the animal was a man-eater. We were appalled. When one leopard looks just the same as another in broad daylight, how could anyone arrive at a considered decision at a moment's notice in the dark? Under pressure from panicky villagers and forest officials desperate to make the problem go away, would he squander an opportunity to kill the animal?

In March 2013, another child was killed in Gauchar, and a leopard was shot dead. Was it the child-lifter? No one knows. It was killed while tucking into a calf.

Would a leopard caught eating a human corpse be guilty of the crime of manslaughter? Leopards are scavengers, frequently feasting on others' kills. Even if a leopard is caught on a corpse, it doesn't prove it killed the person.

Wherever we travelled with Rawat, people hailed him with folded hands, posed for photographs with him, and welcomed him into their homes. He was a local hero.

A forest official requesting anonymity said the department was forced by agitated villagers to kill leopards. On one occasion, eight of his men were doused with kerosene and confined to a room by villagers who threatened to set them on fire if the man-eating leopard wasn't killed. The official had to deal with the situation with no direction from his boss who had switched off his phone. With no space for negotiations, the man said he was forced to sacrifice a leopard. He agreed it was illegal, didn't solve the problem, but at least, it appeased the villagers, who set his staff free.

In Mandi, a cub, said to be the man-eater's, and an adult male leopard were shot dead in separate incidents over the following two weeks. The cub's killing was unjustified, but why was the latter suspected of being a man-eater? It committed the crime of being seen near the site of a human kill.

Everyone—conservationists, villagers, and the forest department—agrees a man-eater has to be removed, but no one can say how to identify one.

Drugging Leopards

A couple of days after the leopard was shot in Mandi, Himachal Pradesh, state forest officials and the hunter who shot the animal claimed they had tried to dart the leopard and failed. A divisional forest officer said the 'hilly terrain and thick bushes make tranquillising next to impossible.'

I talked to wildlife veterinarian Aniruddha Belsare about the challenges of tranquillising wild animals.

'Chemical restraint [restraining an animal with drugs] is a risky procedure,' Dr Belsare said. 'In a hospital for humans with state-of-art facilities and the best doctors, the perils of anaesthesia are explained prior to any procedure, and the family of the patient signs a consent form.'

In the case of free-ranging wild animals, the hazards of chemical restraint escalate. Vets don't know the health status of the animal or its physiological status. They don't have the luxury of running blood tests before the operation to gauge the animal's vital body functions. They don't even know the weight of the animal or if it is pregnant.

Based merely on a visual assessment of the creature from a distance, often getting no more than a glimpse of a flank, they estimate the dosage of drugs.

The drugs are shot from a distance of no more than 10 to 20 metres, using a tranquillising gun or blowpipe. The animal can develop capture myopathy, a fatal condition caused by extreme stress, or it can choke on its vomit. If the animal moves at the critical moment, the dart may hit and damage a vital organ.

Drugs take around fifteen minutes to knock a leopard out. In that time, it can get away, or attack the capture team or a bystander. Sometimes, sedatives may not have the slightest effect on severely stressed animals.

'Since the risks are great, generally, free-ranging animals should not be tranquillized unless it is a dire emergency,' Dr Belsare says. 'Never, never dart a leopard on the loose. It's dangerous. Always trap the animal or corner it in a room before drugging the animal through the bars of the cage or window. I learnt this by nearly getting killed myself.'

Sometimes, an animal may refuse to get trapped, like one leopard suspected of killing six people in Maharashtra. The forest department's innovative idea of luring her to

fall into a dry well worked and they carted her off to a rescue centre.

'Would tranquillisation be impossible under any conditions, like in hilly terrain?' I asked.

'You can always find a way to do it. The real problem is: many vets are skittish about tranquillisation because they fear the risks. Often they trap, move, and handle wild animals without sedating them. Stress, self-inflicted injuries from struggling, or capture myopathy can kill the animal seven to ten days later. Chemical restraint is the most critical tool when dealing with wildlife emergencies. A hundred years ago, we extracted teeth without anaesthesia. Would you go to a dentist who refuses to use drugs today? After all, even local anaesthesia has its perils.'

Had the department succeeded in tranquillising the leopard in Mandi, what next? There are zoos and rescue centres all over the country, operating at full capacity. Not only are the animals expensive to maintain, but they are also no longer part of the cat society and ecosystem. They don't mate, hunt, patrol their territories, or keep the newly independent young ones on their toes. They may be alive in captivity, but for the wilderness, they are dead and gone.

Releasing these animals elsewhere is also dangerous, as they may cause problems in the new area.

While it's easy to offer management instructions from the safety of our homes, what options does the department have if it can't take these animals into captivity, cannot release them, and cannot kill them? That's why it's important to prevent conflict from occurring at all.

Why do Leopards kill Humans?

A leopard on a human-killing spree must be removed immediately. In some places, that doesn't solve the problem permanently. A few months later, another leopard starts hunting again, as the long history of man-eaters in the two neighbouring states of Himachal Pradesh and Uttarakhand shows. The only way to break this cycle of man and animal killing each other is to understand what causes it.

At the end of a four-year-study of leopard attacks on humans in Mandi district, Himachal Pradesh, the site of the recent man-eating tragedy, the Wildlife Institute of India thought they had nailed the causes of man-eating: patchy forests, overgrown weeds, and isolated villages.

How are forest officials to act on this diagnosis? Should they mow weeds and move villages? Even if these actions were practical, would that stop leopards from attacking people? Do other areas with similar features face the same problem? The Mandi study didn't provide answers.

Leopards are among the most adaptable predators. If they lose forests, they live in farmlands. If they lose wild prey, they live on livestock. Leopards are also quick to duck undercover at the first sight of humans. Why would such secretive animals overlook the plentiful livestock and stray dogs and become brazen man-killers?

The prevalent thinking among conservationists and forest department was: wild animals like leopards belong in forests. If they lived in farmlands, it was just a matter of time before they attacked people.

After years of hardly any man-eating incidents, leopards suddenly started targeting people in the verdant valley of Junnar, Maharashtra, where farmers grew sugarcane, maize, and bananas. In 2001, leopards attacked fifty people and killed twenty-nine. The usual speculations were bandied: lack of forest, lack of wild prey animals, disturbance from a dam, and extensive sugarcane fields. But the problem lay elsewhere.

A research project by Kaati Trust uncovered that several months before man-eaters struck, the forest department began a programme of trapping leopards from sugarcane fields and releasing them in the nearest forest. By the time nearly 150 relocations had taken place, attacks on people became frequent. Villagers were nervous wrecks.

Research shows that moving carnivores does not solve the problem of run-ins with humans. For one thing, many animals return to their old haunts within months. Leopards that gave humans a wide berth are traumatized by the capture operation, when hundreds of people yell, poke, pull their tails, and bang the metal bars of the cage. In a desperate attempt to get away, the terrified cats slam against the enclosure, ripping claws, breaking canines, and fracturing skulls.

Released man-eaters attack people in the new area. A leopard suspected of killing seven people in March-April 2013 was trapped on the edge of Tadoba Tiger Reserve and released inside the forest. Within a week, six people in a nearby village were killed.

In Junnar, researchers found that shuffling leopards around the countryside as casually as a deck of cards created man-eaters. Resident leopards were pitted against released ones, and mothers struggled to protect their cubs from strange males. The result? A population of traumatized leopards attacking people.

To live alongside leopards, farmers need help to secure their livestock and know how to avoid leopards. Instead, the well-intentioned department focused its attention on leopards. After all, wildlife laws say protected animals that are a *threat* to human life must be relocated.

The situation returned to normal when sixty-two leopards were taken to permanent captivity. Over time, leopards from the surrounding areas moved in, and today, live in the same farmlands, taking a few heads of livestock but not wilfully attacking people.

Had the Junnar study not been conducted, how would the forest department have resolved the problem? Uprooted sugarcane, planted a forest, and released pigs and deer?

The only way to find a long-term solution is to look beyond conventional wisdom and analyse what causes leopards to attack humans in particular places and not others. Until then, these tragedies will continue.

The Making of a Snake Expert

Ashok Captain's postcards, written in all caps, from Pune, were always about snakes. He asked Rom to identify the creatures he described. The year was 1994, before the Age of Emails.

Rom grew tired of answering his queries and urged him to get a copy of Malcolm A. Smith's *Fauna of British India: Volume III. Serpentes*. The brown hardcover, published in 1943 and reprinted many times over, is a snake specialist's Bible.

Within a few weeks, Ashok learnt how to identify snakes from Smith's book. Anyone reading his postcards would think the messages were in code. One said, 'Sc 15, V 145, A 2, C 54, SL 7 ¾, IL 7-8, T 1+2, LO -. Bands 24+. Oligodon erythrorachis?' This gibberish is how snake-people talk.

Rom had long dreamt of writing an update to Smith's book, complete with colour photographs, so even an amateur could use it. He thought Ashok had achieved adequate proficiency in snake-people talk to be his co-author.

I missed Ashok's first visit to the Croc Bank. 'What's he like?' I asked Rom. 'What does he do?'

'The man is interested in snakes,' his baffled expression appeared to say. 'What else do you want to know?' The truth is, Rom didn't know himself.

When I finally met Ashok months later, I saw a wiry, balding man in his 30s. He'd been a racing cyclist in his youth. His interest in snake identification was sparked because he wanted to label his astoundingly beautiful photographs.

Ashok used multiple flashes and commandeered friends to act as flash-holders. He demanded they stand still as statues, no matter how uncomfortable they were. For their pains, they were paid in pizzas and ice creams. The snakes got nothing, of course.

Once the rolls of film came back from the lab, he scrutinized each transparency. He kept the best one of each species of snake and destroyed the rest. When I protested, he retorted, 'I don't like mediocre.'

Ashok brought his perfectionism to the snake book as well. He spent late nights counting and recounting scales of specimens in the Bombay Natural History Society's museum. When he couldn't sort it out, he contacted the experts.

During the course of writing the book, computers crashed a few times and valuable data was lost. Ashok shrugged off these setbacks with, 'Builds character.'

Ten years after the project began, the manuscript was done. Being a photographer, Ashok was particular about printing quality, and being a snake conservationist, Rom wanted an affordable retail price. The more I overheard them discussing the unsatisfactory terms offered by publishers, the stronger an idea took root.

I had just given up filmmaking and had started writing. There was no way I could pay my bills from my writing income. Perhaps I could turn publisher. I thought I knew the market for snake books, and since I was the boss, I could choose the printer and set the price. Both Rom and Ashok thought I was mad, but the book was done to our satisfaction.

Within a decade, Ashok, a nature enthusiast with no formal training became the foremost expert on snake taxonomy in India, and today has two snake species named in his honour.

In 2008, the host of a wildlife documentary opened the snake book to identify a shieldtail snake shown earlier in the film. I thought it was excellent publicity, as the second edition had arrived fresh from the printers.

When the producer sought permission to use the book in the film, Ashok refused. 'My answer is a flat, absolute "no",' he said. 'It is not possible to identify a shieldtail snake using our field guide.'

Shieldtails are burrowers, and many species look alike; the only way to tell them apart is by counting scales and teeth.

'He'll make us count scales, even to identify obvious snakes like cobras,' I grumbled to myself.

Today, if Rom is uncertain about the identity of a snake, he asks for Ashok's advice. God forbid if Rom has the temerity to send a photograph without scale information.

Fishing for Nothing

Rom dreamed of fighting legendary game fish like snowtrout and chocolate mahseer on the River Kameng, Arunachal Pradesh.

For eight hours every day for about ten days, a group of us rafted down the river. As we drifted down calm stretches, we watched people turn over soil with hoes on steep slopes no draft animals could walk. We joked one leg had to be shorter than the other to work in this terrain. Coming from the plains, I couldn't imagine even walking up those vertical inclines, never mind working all day.

It was 2009, and there were no reminders of modern civilization: electricity, medical care, or telephones.

By mid-afternoon, we pulled ashore, exhausted. While the rest of us set up camp, Rom stalked fish. In these backwoods, he expected the river to be teeming. A couple of hours later, watching him dejectedly approach the camp, I knew he hadn't caught any.

Tired of eating from cans, the support staff hoped Rom

would catch some fish. One afternoon, the cook and his assistant gave him unsolicited advice: his fancy, imported lures and spinners were useless. They pressed a ball of wheat dough in his hand and said, 'Try this.' With nothing to lose, Rom squeezed the damp glob on a hook and set off once again. Not even a nibble.

Every day we heard dull explosions reverberate down the valley. Hundreds of hydroelectric dams were scheduled to be built across the state, and we had already noticed new roads being blasted into hillsides on our way up.

Rom buttonholed a Nyishi man and, through elaborate pantomime, asked what to use as bait. He said insects, but we couldn't figure out what kind. With renewed determination and a fat grasshopper in hand, Rom set off once more. No strike. Did the river have any fish?

The following day, we found small, dead fish bobbing amongst rocks as we drifted downstream. They were all the same species of labeo, an algae-eating carp, with suction pads to cling to rocks in a swift-flowing river.

'Dynamite,' Rom said.

The explosions we heard were not roadworks but lazy, destructive fishermen. They threw a stick of ignited explosive into the river to stun fish and make them float belly up. Larger fish went into the pot, while smaller fish floated downriver, unnecessarily dead.

Had all the other kinds of fish besides the carp been wiped out? We didn't see one leap out of the water to snatch an insect or churn the sandy coast when we sprinkled crumbs.

As we followed the river's course down the hills and

closer to civilization, we passed a construction site. High above us, workers were cutting a road. Earthmovers sent huge boulders bouncing down the slope and splashing into the river, dangerously close to us. We yelled and waved our bright yellow paddles to attract the operators' attention. Finally, one of the bystanders gesticulated at the workers and work stopped long enough for us to row past.

Dynamite intended for road construction was being traded all the way to the interior villages. Had Rom not struggled to catch a fish day after day, we'd have been oblivious to the river's lack of piscine life.

At one of the larger towns, styrofoam boxes of frozen fish were being unloaded from a refrigerated truck at the market. The driver said the fish came from Andhra Pradesh, at least 1,600 kilometres away. Villagers of a state traditionally rich in natural wealth relied on fish brought in by roads that were indirectly causing the ruin of their native fish diversity.

A press release dated 26 August 2013, announced the discovery of a new species of fish from a tributary of the Siang, Arunachal Pradesh. I scanned down the report to see what kind of fish it was. It belonged to the same family of carp we found in the Kameng.

Rom still dreams of angling for snowtrout and mahseer.

Millipede Hunters

Every monsoon brings out millipedes by the thousands; the small black and yellow flat millipedes, the slim brown ones with a red stripe running down their backs, and the large 20-centimetre browns.

As anyone who's stepped on one knows, they smell awful. Millipedes exude cyanide gas and a cocktail of noxious chemicals like benzoquinone to deter predators.

Two years ago, we bought a pair of emu chicks to add to our menagerie, and the breeder warned they were dumb, likely to eat stones, plastic pieces, bits of wire, or anything else. He advised keeping them in an enclosure until they were six months old.

When they were old enough, Rom and I cleaned a paddock of stones, sharp twigs, shards of broken terracotta planters, and wood chips. We let the birds loose and watched as they plucked flowers and picked over dry leaves. Unexpectedly, one chick bolted down a long, snaky thing.

'Did it just eat a millipede?' I asked Rom in horror.

He didn't know; he was watching the other bird. But the millipede assassin seemed none the worse for it.

When a black and yellow flat millipede crossed the path in front of an emu chick, I held my breath. The emu examined it, tilting its head to the side and giving one eye an unhindered view. Shaking its head seemingly with distaste, the bird wandered away. Rom looked at me as if to say, 'You must have been hallucinating.'

A butterfly flew past, and the chicks stumbled after it, their large feet getting in the way. Watching their clumsy and comical antics, I relaxed.

Then one of the emus swallowed a large, brown millipede in plain sight.

'Did you see that?' I demanded.

Rom had, and was concerned.

An hour later, the emu chick still hadn't keeled over. Instead, both of them competitively bolted down the large millipedes like I hog brownies.

I spent that evening on the net and identified the millipede as possibly being *Spinotarsus colosseus*; I named it Colossus for short. Many species of millipedes in Australia, where emus originate, look similar to Colossus. However, not one website mentioned emus eating millipedes. Nor could I find out if Colossus was toxic.

Wedge-capped capuchins of Venezuela and black lemurs of Madagascar use millipedes as ready dispensers of insect repellent. The monkeys nibble on the leggy invertebrates a little, and rub the benzoquinone exuded by millipedes all over their fur to ward off mosquitoes. The chemical is many times more effective than any man-made, DEET-containing, insect repellent.

Benzoquinone makes the primates drool profusely and their eyes glaze over, leading some wildlife documentary producers to speculate that they were getting high.

Although capuchins and lemurs live on two different continents, they use millipedes of the same family, Spirostreptidae, which is closely related to Colossus. I wondered why the emus weren't affected if millipedes were so poisonous.

Colossus millipedes disappeared from the paddock within weeks, while the two other species sedately crawled about. Although these unmolested species were smaller than Colossus, they probably packed a toxic punch. Perhaps, the emus did know what was safe to eat.

In May 2013, we celebrated the emus' second birthday. I was relieved we had no medical emergencies when the Colossus assassins were growing up.

At this time, I had cause for renewed concern. Amba and Chola, our three-month-old puppies, began gobbling up the flat millipedes. Unlike the emus, they breathed that unpleasant crushed millipede stink in our faces. But like the emus, they suffered neither poisoning nor indigestion. Nor do they seem to be getting high. We don't know if these millipedes are hardly toxic, if dogs

and emus are immune to them, or if eating millipedes confers some advantage.

But the pups won't touch Colossus or the red-striped millipede. Perhaps Colossus is far too large for them. While the red millipede may not be named *Xenobolus carnifex* for nothing – *carnifex* means 'public executioner' in Latin!

Holy Crocs

Dhalapahar, the female mugger croc, was at the far end of the large pond, disobeying the caretaker's loud calls. A crowd of pilgrims waited to offer chicken and chunks of mutton. Dhalapahar was more interested in guarding her nest.

Khalapahar, the big male, didn't know how to say 'no', and responded half-heartedly when summoned to consume yet another chicken. Feeding crocodiles is a ritual at the mausoleum of Khan Jahan Ali, the 15th-century Sufi saint and ruler of Bagerhat, Bangladesh. Dhalapahar and Khalapahar were two of the last three remaining mugger crocs in the country.

In 2003, Rom was called to investigate why these reptiles hadn't made babies for fifteen years. As we found out at the Madras Croc Bank, mugger crocs are really scaly rabbits, each female producing at least twenty hatchlings a year. If these animals had trouble making babies, something was radically wrong.

Rom tried to catch Dhalapahar to get her off the nest. She was so fat her neck was wider than her head, and the noose wouldn't stay on. A long struggle later, an exhausted and sweaty Rom trussed her up. After excavating her nest, Rom examined the eggs. None of them had the opaque band that indicates fertility.

When Rom solemnly shook his head with the bad news, a ripple of resentment went through the crowd of *khadem*s, hereditary caretakers of the shrine and its holy crocs, watching the operation. One khadem insisted Khan Jahan Ali would fertilize the eggs at a later date.

Despite the bluster, we knew the khadems were anxious about their impotent mugger. If Khalapahar and Dhalapahar died, the shrine's revenue would suffer. As a conservationist, Rom felt this was a good place to spark a programme to bring muggers back to Bangladesh.

Khalapahar and Dhalapahar were grossly overweight. As in humans, obesity can make crocs impotent. The two crocs had to go on a diet immediately. But pilgrims believe their wishes come true if they feed these crocs. The only way to keep everyone happy was to spread the offerings among many mouths.

Rom offered fifty fertile eggs from Madras Croc Bank to replace Dhalapahar's infertile ones. She was a good mom, and the 60-hectare pond was excellent habitat. Instead of welcoming the ingenious idea, the khadems were vehemently opposed to it.

'Your crocs are heathen,' they said.

'Once the hatchlings drink this water, they'll become blessed,' Rom replied.

Then a khadem said they preferred to artificially

inseminate Dhalapahar rather than bring Madrasi crocs over. At that time, the technique hadn't been successfully used in crocs. For the rest of the day, the debate raged between Rom and a vociferous group of thirty khadems, mediated by a translator. I grew bored of watching this exchange, alternating between science and superstition, and wondered when Rom was going to pull out his trump card.

After dark, we walked around the perimeter of the pond while Rom scanned the water with a spotlight. Suddenly, we heard a splash. Rom waded in to get a clear view, and to our surprise, pinned under the sharp beam of light was a young saltwater crocodile. Apparently, the worried khadems had found another solution.

The following day, Rom went on the offensive. If Madrasi mugger crocs were not holy enough, how could a different species of crocodile be acceptable? He warned that allowing a saltwater croc to live among people was disastrous. The khadems would ignore this advice at their peril.

With the khadems caught on the back foot, Rom finally pulled out the black-and-white photograph taken in 1941 in Karachi, Pakistan. I had been waiting for this moment. A hush descended on the crowd as everyone craned their necks to see over the shoulders of others. The photograph

showed numerous mugger crocs sprawled over each other at Manghopir, a Sufi shrine like Khan Jahan Ali Mazar.

'Your pond could look like that someday,' Rom said softly.

The khadems agreed to take the Madrasi crocs.

After meeting conservationists in Khulna, Rom drafted a plan to bring mugger crocs back to Bangladesh. The Madras Croc Bank would send fifty fertile mugger eggs to Khan Jahan Ali Mazar, and forty adult mugger crocs to zoos.

In January 2005, the female mugger croc Dhalapahar was fatally injured in a fight with Khalapahar. By then, the initial offer to send eggs had been vetoed.

Six months later, forty crocs flew from Chennai to Dhaka, and Khan Jahan Ali Mazar got seven of those reptiles.

After the short consultancy in 2003, to draft a conservation plan, Rom wasn't invited back to implement it. Everything was quiet until August 2008 when a croc killed a twenty-five-year-old man at the Khan Jahan Ali Mazar pond. Within days, a woman was dragged from the water's edge into the pond, but she survived.

I asked our contacts in Bangladesh if the saltwater crocodile (saltie) was still living in the pond.

After making enquiries, a colleague reported the saltie was the culprit.

'It hasn't been removed,' I exclaimed to Rom as I slapped my forehead.

By then, the five-foot-croc would have reached ten feet in length, a dangerous size for an aggressive species to live among people. Back in 2003, Rom had warned the khadems that the saltie was a threat to human life.

But another colleague suggested mugger crocs from India were to blame. He said these weren't the first attacks. In March 2008, two people were attacked and one was killed. Since that was mugger breeding season, could the victims have blundered into a protective mother croc's nest site?

There was more bad news. In April, two khadems viciously beat a nesting mugger, blinding her in one eye and severely injuring a leg. Were they teaching it a lesson for attacking humans?

A crocodile farmer said since the female croc stayed close to her nest and refused to obey calls to feed, pilgrims were leaving their offerings with a khadem who lived nearby. This upset other khadems who tried to chase the croc away from her nest by beating her up. By the time we heard of the incident a few months later, the croc's leg had healed.

Rom and I felt bad; these were our crocs being mistreated. They had known nothing but security at the Croc Bank. There was little we could do without being formally asked. Ideally, one of the conservation plan's key strategies— conducting awareness programmes for the khadems and other residents of the area—should have been done. Local conservationists raised funds to erect signboards cautioning people of crocodiles. But nobody attempted to remove the saltie, despite repeated warnings.

In November 2009, a news report said two men were sentenced to two years in prison for trashing the nesting crocodile.

After a respite, the attacks started again. A woman was killed in June 2011, and two people were injured in July. A news report said some khadems had sent a petition to the deputy commissioner of the area, demanding the removal of mugger crocs from the pond. They claimed the crocs of Indian origin were aggressive.

Another group of khadems filed a counter-petition against the removal of crocs and accused some khadems of misappropriating money meant for feeding the crocs. These starving crocs were attacking pilgrims, they alleged. Ironically, the news report showed a picture of an obese mugger. After hearing both sides, the district administration decided not to move the crocs. No one mentioned the saltie.

In October that year, the saltie was beaten to death. I couldn't help thinking: the road to this conservation hell is paved with our good intentions.

Since then, there have been no reports of crocodile attacks, and we can only hope the khadems treat the mugger crocs humanely.

The Obsession Effect

Steve Gooder placed the round bottle on our dining table with a flourish and said, 'And you'll need this.' I watched the amber liquid sloshing inside the bottle before reading the large letters: Obsession for Men.

'Why would we need that?' I asked.

'It works like a charm on cats.'

I looked at him sceptically.

He raised his eyebrows and tilted his head as if to say, 'Trust me.'

Steve, a wildlife documentary producer, was visiting us to discuss a film on leopards. The story pivoted around the one prowling our neighbourhood, and he wanted a video recording of it.

He brought twelve video camera traps that filmed by infrared light, invisible to humans and most animals. He instructed us to spray the men's eau de toilette around the cameras to lure the leopard.

Every evening, Rom and his assistant, Vineet, spent an

hour rigging these traps all over the farm and baiting each with Obsession for Men by Calvin Klein.

Rom and I eschewed strong smelling personal products. They are olfactory beacons in the forest, giving our presence away. It seemed counter-intuitive to spray these human-use products to attract cats.

Every morning, the two men retrieved the camera traps, and we examined the images to see what the night had brought. There were porcupines, jungle cats, spotted civets, palm civets, but no leopard.

Within a week, I couldn't walk on the path without thinking, 'This farm reeks of a masculine bordello.'

One morning, Rom and I were amused to see a palm civet repeatedly mating with a female on camera. Is this why humans wear perfume? To act as aphrodisiacs for local wildlife? If this was the Obsession effect, then it was just a matter of time before the leopard made an appearance. No such luck.

Steve sent desperate sounding emails. Where was the leopard? Were we spraying the cologne?

I was intrigued by his confidence in the men's fragrance. According to the description, the 'scent is a compelling blend of botanical, spices and rare woods.' Why would cats be attracted to these vegetarian smells?

But Steve wasn't alone in trusting the scent. Scientists in Guatemala and Nicaragua used it to successfully lure jaguars. A pair of these elusive cats even mated on camera, like our palm civets.

Besides botanical fragrances, the men's perfume also contains civetone, the musk secretion of civets. Now I understood why the palm civets were going at it. Today, the perfume industry doesn't rely on these anal secretions of animals but instead uses a synthetic version made from palm oil.

But why would large, 100-kilogram jaguars and 60-kilogram leopards be affected by the territorial markings of 5-kilogram civets? Did wild leopards go into paroxysms of pleasure sniffing spotted civet markings? The last thing prey animals want to do is attract predators. This didn't make sense.

Our leopard missed his chance of becoming a television star. Steve finished the film by downplaying his role, but we wondered what became of the cat. A couple of months after *Leopards: 21st Century Cats* premiered in the UK, he sauntered by, triggering one of the cameras.

Was our leopard averse to the come-hither perfume?

In 2005, Pat Thomas, general curator at Bronx Zoo, New York, tested twenty-four well-known men's and women's perfumes on captive and wild cats. Bored captive cheetahs spent more time rubbing their cheeks against spots sprayed with Obsession than any other perfume. The alien scent challenged the cats' ownership of territory, and the animals reclaimed it by rubbing their own scents.

However, in a game reserve in South Africa, lions, leopards, and cheetahs, like our neighbourhood cat, ignored the perfumes. Perhaps they were used to tourists and their smells.

Rom came to dinner one evening smelling of Obsession. What did he think I was: a bored captive cheetah or a wild cat?

Sibling Wars

From the moment I brought home a litter of German shepherd puppies, Cleo singled out one for special treatment. The mongrel's hackles rose whenever she saw Koko, although she had no trouble accepting the rest. She growled menacingly until Koko whimpered and peed in fright. I yelled at Cleo to lay off, but she disobeyed.

When I returned home from shopping, my mother said Cleo had peed on Koko. I felt bad for the puppy. We divided the garden with chain link. Koko and her siblings on one side, and the two older dogs, Cleo and Pokhiri, on the other. There were no further issues between Cleo and Koko, and I was complacent. However, in solving a small problem, I created a bigger one.

When Koko's brother, Karadi, matured, he and Pokhiri savaged each other through the gaps in the chain link. Except for Karadi, all the dogs had been fixed. Should I neuter Karadi? But the vet said we had waited too long, and it wouldn't make any difference to the conflict now.

To prevent the boys from seeing each other, we covered the fence with palm fronds.

One afternoon, Karadi busted through a gate and both dogs fought viciously. I screamed and beat them with my slippers, but they seemed more intent on killing each other. Eventually, during a break in the fight, I got between them and beat Karadi back to his side of the fence. When it was over, not only did the two dogs have bloody lacerations and swollen faces, but I suffered deep puncture wounds on my arms.

When Rom came home, I burst into tears. The physical wounds didn't hurt as much as seeing my beloved dogs fighting each other like demons. I wanted them all to get along with each other so we could be one happy family.

Reading a bunch of dog behaviour books reminded me of the friction between my brother and me. I remembered my father driving a five-year-old me to the hospital the morning after my brother was born.

On the drive, father asked, 'What shall we name your brother?'

'Nothing,' I replied.

Father tried once more, 'Don't you want a baby brother?'

'No.'

Throughout the time we spent under our parents' roof, my brother and I bickered over every little thing. He ran to our parents for support, and they chided me, 'He's younger than you. You should adjust.' Not only was I annoyed with him for complaining to our parents, but I was also irritated that whatever the problem, I had to back off.

I learnt much from the dog books that may as well be

parenting lessons. Most importantly, the initial aggression between older and younger dogs should run its course. The dominant ones want to ensure new entrants know who the top dogs are.

Secondly, during these face-offs, owners should support the older dogs. By rushing to Koko's defence, I undermined Cleo's status, just as my parents had made me insecure. We are naturally protective of the youngest, making this the toughest lesson to practice.

None of this told me how to take down the fence that separated the dogs. I could let them meet on neutral territory to get to know each other. But I was too chicken to try it. Both Pokhiri and Karadi were powerful dogs, and I wasn't confident I could handle them if they went for each other's throats. The fence stayed.

When a leopard took Karadi, his siblings took over the territorial war. Cobras and tick-borne disease took their toll until only Koko remained. I adopted more puppies, and when Koko growled and threatened them, I ignored her. I learnt to trust she didn't mean harm. The little ones rolled on their backs and exposed their bellies in submission. Koko was appeased, and everyone got along as adults.

Many years later, after Cleo and Pokhiri died, the fence came down, finally.

Rom and the King

Rom was walking along a forest path in Agumbe, Karnataka, in May 1972, when he saw a black tail disappear into some bushes. His brain screamed, 'Ratsnake!' Without a moment's hesitation, he dove, bruising elbows and knees, but he had the tail. An instant later, he heard a deep growl. Rom looked up only to see a king cobra, with an expanded hood, towering over him.

The snake's golden hood was iridescent in the evening light, and its eyes were pinned on Rom. Lying flat on his belly, Rom was incapable of defending himself. The king cobra's glossy tail fell from his fingers, and the snake slid away like mercury through the undergrowth.

Coming to his senses and feet, Rom raced after it. He seized a stick and halted the snake in its track. When he grabbed it by the tail a second time, the king cobra swung around and charged open-mouthed. Somehow, holding the snake at a safe distance with the stick, Rom managed, one-handed, to pull a sleeping bag out of his rucksack, and prop it open with sticks. The frightened snake saw the dark opening of the bag as an escape and slid inside. That first knee-quaking encounter with a wild king cobra was not only a career milestone for Rom, but he felt he came of age then.

As a schoolboy in Kodaikanal, Rom devoured *Snakes of the World* by Raymond Ditmars, a herpetologist at Bronx Zoo, New York. He read king cobras were the longest venomous snakes in the world, growing up to 18 feet in length, and he was smitten. At age thirteen, size mattered as well as the danger.

While hiking below Kodaikanal, Rom visited the natural history museum at Sacred Heart College, Shenbaganur. Amongst bottles of preserved animals, he was excited to see the preserved head of a king cobra. He hadn't known he was in king cobra land. He spent his free time during his remaining school years trekking through the forests of the Palni Hills but didn't find the snake of his dreams.

The first live king cobra Rom ever saw wasn't in India but in Florida. In 1963, Rom went to work at Bill Haast's Miami Serpentarium.

Rom watched in awe when Bill took one of the 16-footers out, and the snake stood up high enough to stare him in the eyes. Bill distracted the king cobra with one hand while grabbing it swiftly behind the head with the other. The crowd of tourists never failed to gasp at the swift manoeuvre, and Rom never tired of watching the snakes. While their size was impressive, Rom was intrigued that these snakes seemed more aware of their surroundings. Unlike other snakes, king cobras appeared to be intelligent.

When Rom returned to India in 1967, he was determined to see a wild king cobra. Writer Kenneth Anderson suggested he hunt around Agumbe. On the first day of Rom's first visit to Agumbe in 1972, he leapt on a wild king cobra.

A couple of days later, he caught a female, and brought both snakes to Madras where they made many babies.

While Rom knew a lot about rearing king cobras in captivity, their lives in the wild remained a mystery. For many years, he couldn't entice academic herpetologists to collaborate. They feared there were too few king cobras for a study. Finally, Rom convinced Matt Goode of the University of Arizona that numbers were not a concern. They tagged five king cobras with radios to study their lives in the wild, in Agumbe. It was path-breaking work—the first such study of the species in the world and of any snake in India. After just four years, the research project wound up, not from lack of king cobras but lack of state-issued research permits.

While Rom got a glimpse into the lives of wild king cobras, I still don't understand one thing. Even allowing for hormone-charged, super-human capabilities, how did Rom bag that snake with one hand without getting bitten?

Fatherly Love

The mugger crocodile dug into the sand with her stubby forelegs. Rom and I watched her silently with our chins and arms resting on the enclosure wall. The moon was obscured by clouds, and the Madras Crocodile Bank was in darkness. Bright white torchlight disturbs animals, so we had covered ours with a transparent red film. Mosquitoes complained around our heads, unable to alight on repellent-sprayed skin.

When the pile of sand the croc had dug started to pour back into the hole, her hind legs heaved it off the site, raining sand on her spouse. The large bull croc that lay submerged in water, blinked a few times, and continued to watch the proceedings.

My legs began to tire from standing, and I wished the reptile would hurry up. When she heaved again, a white blob flew out and landed on the slope. A sand-crusted hatchling hung out of the eggshell, squawking in a small nasal voice. Instead of going to the little fellow's aid, mama croc probed the hole with her snout, picked up two eggs, and rolled them gingerly in her jaws. A chorus of baby squawks answered the first hatchling's cry. Then the bull croc crawled up the slope.

'What's he going to do?' I whispered urgently to Rom.

'Don't know.'

The croc picked up the hatchling in distress, carried it to the water, and chomped a couple of times.

'Is he eating it?' I was stricken with horror.

Free of its eggshell, it swam daringly near the large croc's head. Leaving the little fellow bobbing in the water, the father turned around and climbed up the sandbank all the way to the nest. He butted the female croc, who was half his size, out of the way and picked up babies and eggs from the nest. One hatchling's head was caught between the conical teeth, while its body dangled in mid-air. It waved its legs awkwardly, but dad didn't notice. He slid down the bank, propelled by his forelegs.

With the big chap out of the way, the mother went back to work. But daddy croc was having none of it. He chased her away and ferried more babies to the water until the nest was empty. I was touched by the bloke's concern for his offspring and how gently he picked up the little ones.

The following morning, we visited the enclosure to see the family. About twenty-five hatchlings were resting in the shallows in the shade. Dad was in attendance, guarding them against crows, egrets, and herons. Mother was also in the water but at a distance. The staff of the Madras Crocodile Bank gathered to watch this marvel of a hands-on father.

In the Chambal, researchers from the Croc Bank are

studying gharial behaviour. A dominant male gharial probably fathers almost all the babies born in his territory. Come hatching time, hundreds of offspring from many nests gather together in one large crèche guarded by dad. He may be a macho male with white battle scars on his face, but he allows the hatchlings to take great liberties. They pile up on his head, eyes, and nose, the safest perch to catch the sun's rays. He even indulges them with joy rides. But should a threat appear, he roars forward, rudely scattering his babies in the water. They swim ashore, while dad showboats up and down the river.

It's not just the muggers and gharials who make such caring fathers. When Siamese croc babies hatch at the Croc Bank, they cluster at the far end of the pond, away from tourists. When the parents are fed, the hatchlings nibble on any titbit that floats their way. If the breeze blows the piece away from them, the father picks it up, and drops it in front of the little ones. Over the course of an afternoon, he may ferry the meat chunk numerous times.

Crocodilian fathers have been tender gender benders long before humans came up with the term.

Fruit-eaters

Crocodiles and alligators eat meat: red and white, fresh and bloody, or rotten and stinky. When croc biologists noticed seeds in the stomachs of dead crocs and excreted in croc poo, they were dismissive. The reptiles eat fruit-eaters and herbivores, and the seeds most likely came from the preys' stomachs. Even when they found seeds of sixteen species in 265 alligator stomachs, biologists collectively labelled it 'plant material'.

Some witnessed crocs eating floating fruit. Perhaps the animals mistook them for insects, the scientists reasoned. They didn't wonder why reptiles with a superb sense of smell and taste gobble up fruit. Then researchers from Brazil reported that captive, broad-snouted caimans ate the fruit of a creeper. They surmised insects buzzing around the fruit might have attracted the crocodiles that inadvertently chomped the whole thing. But the caimans readily ate insect-free fruit. Did the reptiles learn to eat 'plant material' from their fruit-eating enclosure mates, tegu lizards?

In 2002, John Brueggen of St. Augustine Alligator Farm, Florida, reported that both American and Chinese gators ate romaine lettuce and yellow squash. When elderberries were in fruit, they ate whole mouthfuls. Some plucked kumquats directly off trees and chomped them up. Brueggen wondered if captive crocs suffered from nutritional deficiency which made them eat seemingly unnatural croc food.

Last year, Tom Dacey, the executive officer of the International Union for Conservation of Nature's Crocodile Specialist Group, noted that a wild Siamese croc ate a watermelon in Lao PDR.

How widespread is fruit-eating among crocodilians?

Sifting through croc literature, a group of eight American biologists found that of the eighteen species of crocodilians, thirteen had fleshy fruit, berries, nuts, legumes, and grains in their stomachs. In a report published in August 2013, they said as many as eleven studies on American alligators alone recorded plant material in the animals' guts. Among their favourite fruit is the alligator apple, related to custard apple. Other sought-after fruits include passion fruit, squash, and prickly pear. According to villagers in Belize, Morelet's and American crocodiles eat alligator pears, also called avocados, and alligator apples.

Do any Indian species of crocodiles go on a fruit-eating binge?

A 1915 report claimed mugger ate rice grains. In 1938, Humayun Abdulali, an ornithologist, wrote of a mugger eating fallen figs. Saltwater crocodiles had unidentified seeds in their gut.

Crocs aren't the only carnivores to eat fruit. Jackals eat peanuts, jujube, dates, and jamun. In Gujarat, a pair of leopards is said to have destroyed sixty watermelons in a field in one night. Brown palm civets live on a predominantly fruit diet, earning it the distinction of being one of the most frugivorous (fruit-eating) carnivores in the world. 'Frugivorous carnivore' sounds like a contradiction.

Carnivores are meat-eaters. But the scientific classification of life forms includes an order of mammals called Carnivora, a huge group of weasels, civets, dogs, cats, bears, mongooses, and seals. The distinguishing character is not what they eat, but the presence of claws, canines, and molars. While most of them are carnivores, a few are exceptions like bamboo-eating giant pandas.

In 1946, a 13-foot python lay under a mango tree in a tea estate in Siliguri, swallowing a mango. Labourers killed the snake and found four more mangoes in its gut. On looking closer, they found each fruit had two or three insect larvae, the presumed reason for the python to prey on fruit.

Knowing what we do about crocodiles and alligators, maybe the python loved mangoes.

My Personal Trainers

Toro, our Rottweiler-German Shepherd, whom Rom calls a Rotten Shepherd, refused to eat. Worried, I called the vet. Instead of prescribing pills, she asked, 'How much do you walk him every day?'

I hesitated. Since our dogs live on a farm and are not cooped up like city dogs, I didn't think they needed to be walked.

'I don't walk him,' I answered. 'He runs around the yard with Koko all day. Isn't that enough?'

'That's not enough. You have to walk him for 30 minutes at least every day,' she advised.

That evening, we walked the dogs around the farm. I felt like a doofus and hoped our farmer-neighbours wouldn't see us. After we returned, Toro gobbled up his chow.

I don't know what was so enjoyable about going around the farm on leashes, but the dogs insisted we go every day.

Since we began walking the dogs, I noticed my short temper grew a longer fuse. Is that why dogs that spend a long time without exercising are quick to bite? The vet said it certainly makes them neurotic. Do humans who don't exercise suffer the same fate? Apparently so ... with stress, dementia, and depression taking their toll.

Walking was fine until Lola, a Chippiparai, joined the pack. A hunting hound, she needed much more exercise than the others. How do I exercise her without wiping myself out? I trained her to fetch a ball. After the third fetch, she refused to play.

A friend suggested I get a mechanical rabbit for Lola to chase. But the devices cost at least $500. I did the next best thing: I tied a rag mouse to a long rope and dragged it across the garden. Lola sprinted after it. But I grew tired of running around with the rag, while she barely panted.

I thought of building a manually operated mechanical rabbit, turning a wheel would spool the rope while pulling the rag mouse. But I'd still have to walk across the garden to place the mouse and run back to turn the wheel. I would get more exercise than Lola, and that just wouldn't do.

Rom bought a mountain bicycle for me. I was to cycle and Lola would trot along. Great idea, but how to make it work? I rode and whistled for her, but she was content to sit with Rom and watch from the veranda. I lured her

with treats. She came half way and returned. I pulled the rag mouse behind me. That worked until the rope snagged in the wheel, and I fell off the cycle. But I wasn't about to give up.

I held Lola's leash as I cycled. I imagined she had no choice but to run along. I was wrong. When she realized I had succeeded in making her run, she adamantly sat down. I fell down again, and barely avoided breaking my teeth. Cycling wasn't working; there was no choice but to run myself.

We set up a routine of jogging around the farm before the sun rises and heats up the world. The momentum of a daily habit sees me through most days, but when it's disrupted, inertia sets in.

I look for excuses to not stir out of bed so early. I groggily mutter, 'I worked hard yesterday; I need more rest.' But the dogs refuse to pay heed; they have become health freaks. Even if I've had a late night and dark circles under my eyes, the merciless beasts bark me out of bed and prance around while I pull on my shoes. It's all very well for them to be so enthusiastic: when we return, they flop down and go to sleep, but I have to get to work.

After dogs domesticated humans to look after their every need, they have now become self-appointed personal trainers.

Chronicle of a Tsunami Foretold

Could animals have warned us of the 2004 tsunami before it occurred? That was the question many reporters asked Rom in the weeks following the disaster.

On that fateful morning, when giant waves hit the East coast, about 20 kilometres away, our dogs lay asleep under the dining table, while Rom and I bustled about the kitchen.

Rom replied he had seen no evidence of animals' ability to foretell natural disasters. But the reporters quoted eyewitness reports of deer, elephants, buffaloes, and monkeys running to higher ground; bats and flamingos flying away; and zoo animals refusing to leave their shelters.

When Rom wasn't impressed, they demanded, 'Why were there no animal casualties?' One reporter even insisted ants crawled upwards. Rom replied mockingly, 'Really? I've never heard of anything like that.'

Animals certainly have keener senses than we do. Elephants, for instance, are known to sense very low frequency sounds with their feet. But can they feel the ground tremors of earthquakes and tsunamis before they hit? Crucially, do they know what evasive action to take?

How close must animals be to the epicentre of the earthquake to detect them? Do all animals in that radius detect these vibrations? Or are some animals more gifted than others in predicting imminent catastrophes? Hundreds of dogs that washed up dead on the beaches of Phuket, just 450 kilometres from the epicentre, apparently had no premonition at all, while two dogs in Galle, Sri Lanka, more than 1,500 kilometres away, seemingly knew what was coming and refused to go for a walk on the beach.

Even if we know which animals to observe, how do we interpret a specific animal behaviour to mean 'earthquake imminent' and not 'my stomach's cramping' or 'I don't want to go for a walk?' Did an earthquake ensue every time the dogs refused to go for a walk?

It's even more difficult to gauge wild animal behaviour. We need to know what they were doing before the event, if we are to decipher the significance of their post-event actions. Such opportunities are extremely rare.

In Yala National Park, Sri Lanka, scientists Eric Wickramanayake, Peter Leimgruber, and Prithviraj Fernando had radio-collared an adult cow elephant from a herd of about thirty. The transmitter sent the elephant's location coordinates via satellite every four hours. At 2 a.m. on 26 December 2004, the cow elephant and her herd were close to the coast, just 280 metres from the water's edge. At 10 a.m., an hour after the first wave of tsunami struck, the animals were by the beach. They then ambled inland, but returned to the coast the following morning.

Later, when the biologists visited the site, they realized the elephant herd had been on the leeside of a sand dune and was therefore unaffected by the sea's unusual intrusion into land.

Looking at the herd's movements over the preceding days, the biologists concluded it didn't panic and take flight either before, during, or after the tsunami. Did the animals not feel the vibrations of the earthquake and the tsunami? Didn't they think the tidal waves were dangerous?

Many months earlier, the cow elephant was captured, collared, and released. She and her herd were so spooked by the experience, they walked 10 kilometres that night. Clearly, in the animals' estimation, the tsunami was nothing to get worked up about compared to the stress of being captured.

The GPS locations of the elephant's movements are logged for anyone to see. There is no way of independently confirming the eyewitness and hearsay accounts of animals reacting with insight even before the disaster occurred.

In the days following the tsunami, no one took time off to assess the loss of non-human life. While doing humanitarian work, Manori Gunawardena, an elephant biologist, recalls seeing numerous animal carcasses along the Yala coast. Perhaps reporters hadn't looked hard enough.

Despite their inability to warn us of the tsunami, my dogs predict people will continue to believe any story of animals' extraordinary powers of premonition.

Feeding Birds

In Massachusetts, I discovered the wonder of hummingbirds. Tiny and iridescent, they hovered at a feeder just outside the window where Rom and I lay in bed watching them. Determined to create a similar experience at our home in rural Tamil Nadu, I bought a bird feeder.

I reconstituted the feed, following instructions on the package, hung the bottle under the eaves, and waited for sunbirds, the nectar-drinking Old World relatives of hummingbirds. For a few days, nothing happened.

Early one morning, the hummingbird feeder was empty. Sunbirds weren't creatures of the night. At dusk, I watched the refilled feeder from our living room window to catch the slurper. A bat flew from the garden, landed on the bottle, and as the bottle swayed back and forth, quaffed down the red liquid in minutes. I brought the feeder in every evening and hung it out early the following morning. By the time I ran out of hummingbird feed, I had failed to attract a single sunbird.

Since then, I realized feeding animals creates monsters. Hand-fed wild monkeys think of people as ready food-dispensers. They regularly scratch and bite the hands that don't feed them. Buses stop along our road and passengers feed monkeys that have become wayside fixtures. After the vehicles leave, the animals dart across the road to scrounge leftovers, causing automobile accidents and their own deaths.

Pilgrims to Sithulpahuwa shrine in Yala National Park, Sri Lanka, feed wild elephants. These giants lose their fear of humans, and a few have been shot dead in recent years (see *Why did Raja die?*).

Ecologist Rauf Ali said a bull elephant stands on the Joda-Barbil road along Orissa's border with Jharkhand, demanding bananas from passing trucks. On YouTube, I watched the handsome tusker sniff inside trucks, his entire trunk disappearing inside the cab and pulling down sacks from the roof carrier. He was nicknamed RTO by the truck drivers and he has killed four people. But in each case, the forest department decided the elephant wasn't at fault.

Iguanas are harmless, and even if humans fed them, there is little likelihood the reptiles would chase or bite them. So what could possibly be wrong with feeding them? In the Bahamas, tourists feed grapes and ground beef to these herbivorous animals. Many rock iguanas suffer diarrhoea, high cholesterol, and parasites.

Feeding mammals and reptiles has such disastrous consequences. Does feeding birds cause any problems? In Portal, Arizona, a popular birding destination, a resident complained of rattlesnakes colonizing her garden. One of our friends, a snake expert, was called to help. Seed from the bird feeder spilled on the ground, attracting rats and squirrels. The fat rodents drew rattlesnakes like magnets.

In the West, opinion is divided. Some say bird feeding gives people enjoyment, connects them with nature, and aids bird conservation. Others say feeding delays migration, impacts chick production and spreads disease.

Everyone agrees feeding has a big impact on bird survival and reproduction, but there is little information to suggest if it helps or harms birds in the long run. We know even less about the consequences of feeding tropical birds.

Even though I was aware feeding may cause problems, I really wanted sunbirds outside our windows. I convinced myself one little bottle couldn't have a major impact. I wrote to Bikram Grewal, an authority on birds, for advice on suitable food. Instead of answering my question, he suggested planting ixora and hibiscus plants. I wanted to hang artificial feeders, and he was adamant I shouldn't. Left with no choice, I planted flowering plants.

Watching sunbirds flit from flower to flower, I've come around to Bikram's way of thinking. The birds had no difficulty finding the flowers, nor did they have to compete with bats. Best of all, the feed was natural and not artificial sugar water. Besides, flowers are prettier than plastic-capped bottles.

Cat Bait

I felt the farm was an unsafe home after a leopard moved in and ate my dog. A biologist friend advised if I didn't want to invite the cat's attention again, I'd have to get rid of my pets. That was not an option. In that case, the kennel had to be far from the house, she said. I wobbled my head non-committally, but in my mind, I trashed the impractical suggestion. Rom and I had to figure this out on our own.

Leopards kill by biting the throat and crushing the windpipe until the animal suffocates. Shepherds in Maharashtra, Uttarakhand, and Himachal Pradesh protect their dogs with broad metal collars bristling with sharp spikes. These collars would do the trick.

It was only when they arrived that I realized they were lethal. Our dogs could rip their paws before they got used to them. Nor were our shins and hands safe when we played with the dogs. What were a few injuries when lives could be saved?

For centuries, leopards in those northern states had

encountered dogs wearing
these metal collars and learnt
to give them a wide berth.
Would a south Indian
leopard that had never
experienced these collars
leave our dogs alone? What
if it disembowelled our pets
in its attempt to kill them?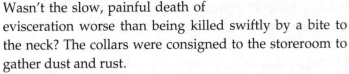
Wasn't the slow, painful death of
evisceration worse than being killed swiftly by a bite to
the neck? The collars were consigned to the storeroom to
gather dust and rust.

In the US, hunters use dogs to chase cougars up trees.
If our dogs knew how to tree the leopard, perhaps they
could escape becoming prey. At three years of age, they
were too old to be trained, and if they didn't learn their
lessons well, they could get killed.

Should I get puppies to train? Not all puppies make
good treeing dogs, and the training process lasts two years.
Besides, I hadn't heard of any instances of dogs treeing
leopards. I didn't want to experiment with our dogs' lives
with an untested idea.

What we did, however, was clip the lower branches of
all trees not only for a clear view of the garden from the
house, but also to make sure there were no hiding spots
for the large cats.

We kept the dogs indoors, either in the house or the
adjoining kennel, day and night. Before letting them out,
we looked around carefully so the dogs didn't blunder
into the jaws of the waiting beast.

When I took the dogs for a walk or a run every morning, I couldn't shake the feeling I was trawling for leopards. But pets needed their exercise and can't be cooped up all the time.

'If the leopard grabs a dog, let it take it,' Rom warned me. 'If you try to protect the dog, the leopard might turn on you.'

I nodded, hoping never to face that eventuality.

Rom returned from Ethiopia with a metal spearhead, used by a tribal community to hunt leopards. After fixing the sharp blade on to a long wooden shaft, he presented it to me to carry on my walks. It was heavy and unwieldy. My father then dried a length of bamboo and straightened it with fire. And this made a light-weight shaft for the spear.

On a trial run, I held the leashes of three dogs in one hand and the spear in the other. To an outsider, I might have looked like I was going on a hunt, but I was trying not to be hunted. The weapon snagged on branches, and I inadvertently whacked a dog or two. I feared I might clumsily spear a dog, jab my foot, or trip on it. Even if I grew used to carrying a spear, I'd probably not use it when the occasion arose.

Every day for the past six years, the dogs and I were out in leopard country, relying on nothing more than our wits to avoid a confrontation. And we survived.

An Appeal to Nature

Section 377 of the Indian Penal Code criminalizes sexual activities 'against the order of nature,' even if conducted voluntarily with man, woman, or animal.

A number of political and religious leaders claim homosexuality is unnatural and welcomed the Supreme Court judgment. Lesbian-Gay-Bisexual-Transgender activists rebut it by citing references to animal homosexuality to prove its naturalness.

There are two issues here: is homosexuality natural? Should nature be the guiding force of human behaviour?

Section 377, drafted in 1860, has its roots in Victorian English morality and understanding of nature. Sex was thought to be mainly for procreation, and any form of non-reproductive sex was taboo.

For many years, biologists didn't report homosexual behaviour in animals because they were embarrassed or didn't want to be embroiled in controversy. Dr George Murray Levick, a surgeon and officer in the British

Antarctic Expedition of 1910, was so scandalized by the homosexual behaviour of Adélie penguins, he wrote a part of his notes in code in the Greek alphabet. Only 100 copies of his manuscript, *Sexual Habits of the Adélie Penguin*, were printed for private circulation and expressly marked in bold typeface: 'Not for Publication.'

Even though biologists continue to have a rough time when they report same-sex behaviour in animals, we now know such behaviour is widespread. Almost every creature that reproduces sexually also performs same-sex.

But assuming anything that occurs in the animal kingdom is good is a slippery slope. Devising laws based on this fallacy is worse.

Orangutans, penguins, and a whole lot of other animals rape. Large cats kill their own kind. Mallard ducks commit necrophilia. These are all arguably natural, basic instincts. But we abhor such behaviour.

Many people adopt others' children, a rare event in the animal world. Some birds have to be tricked into incubating and rearing cuckoo chicks.

Perhaps we shouldn't look at the entire animal kingdom, but instead examine our closest primate relatives, bonobos.

Bonobos hardly ever fight within a troop or declare war against a neighbouring one. They resolve any potential

conflict-prone situation with sex. Sex can be female-female, male-female, or male-male. All members of the species are bisexual.

Yet, the widespread conflict in most human societies makes us seem aggressive, like chimpanzees. Is one of these behaviours more artificial than the other?

Which animal sends its children to school? Does any animal leave its home range to travel to another side of the planet to reside for weeks in a contrived ritual called holiday? No animal looks after its old, weak, and non-productive parents and grandparents, nor does any creature practice contraception and abortion. Are these unique behaviours artificial and contrived? Should they be criminalized?

Clearly, there are some condemnable natural acts and some laudable unnatural ones. Can we infer moral lessons from nature? No. The natural-as-good label may be appropriate for shampoos but not for the way we behave.

Humans aren't extra-terrestrials. We share an evolutionary heritage with other living creatures on this planet. When homosexuality and bisexuality occur widely in nature, it is no surprise it occurs in humans as well.

According to the ninth edition of Black's *Law Dictionary*, 'nature' is: '(1) A fundamental quality that distinguishes one thing from another; the essence of something. (2) A wild condition, untouched by civilization. (3) A disposition or personality of someone or something. (4) Something pure or true as distinguished from something artificial or contrived. (5) The basic instincts or impulses of someone or something.'

Do same-sex relationships exist in the wild, untouched by

civilization? Yes. Is homosexuality artificial or contrived? No. Is homosexuality a basic instinct or disposition for some? Yes. Then, how can anyone conclude homosexuality is against the order of nature?

No animal is homophobic. So, if anything is against the order of nature, it's homophobia.

Why did Homosexuality Evolve?

Same-sex behaviour is well-documented in more than 500 species of animals and birds. For as long as humans have lived, homosexuality has occurred in every culture. If the point of sex is procreation, why has evolution not weeded out non-productive sex?

The Laysan albatross is the epitome of monogamy, with the pair committed to each other for the long haul. But biologists discovered that about 60 per cent of the population in Oahu, Hawaii, is female, and during the breeding season, about 30 per cent of the pairs are female-female.

When there are too few males to go around, many females have no options to reproduce. A female albatross lays only one egg a year, and it takes two birds to incubate it successfully. Some females opt for an alternate strategy. They mate on the sly with males who already have partners, and incubate their eggs with their female partners.

These same-sex pairs perform typical courtship rituals:

rubbing necks, kissing with their bills, and even mounting one another. In 2007, Brenda Zaun, a state biologist, reported that one same-sex relationship lasted nineteen years on the neighbouring island of Kauai.

So is same-sex behaviour merely a response to a short supply of one gender?

Biologists speculate that female-female pairings in Laysan albatrosses continue even when the sex ratio evens out. The birds are the archetype of monogamy, after all, even if the pairs are same-sex.

Male dolphins form brotherhoods and goose each other to cement their relationships. The better they bond, the more effective their coalitions, and they enjoy better access to females.

Is it about improving one's chances of mating with the opposite sex?

Much to the concern of sheep farmers, about 8 per cent of all rams are homosexual, refusing to mate with ewes. These ram-preferring rams have a smaller hypothalamus, the part of the brain that controls reproductive functions, than heterosexual rams.

Although same-sex behaviour appears to be genetic in fruit flies, no gene for gayness has been found in mammals. Intriguingly, identical human twins share the same genetic material, but they don't always share the same sexual orientation.

Some scientists say there is definitely a genetic bias as homosexuality runs in families. Gay men have more gay uncles than heterosexual men. However, this doesn't hold true for lesbians.

An Italian study discovered the mothers, aunts, and

grandmothers of gay men bore more children. A similar study of the Samoan families of *fa'afafine*, a tradition-sanctioned third gender of effeminate men, corroborated these findings. Whatever made the women good at producing babies appeared to modify the sexual orientation of some sons.

In December 2012, a team led by William Rice, an evolutionary biologist at University of California, Santa Barbara, theorized that epigenetic marks might hold the answer. Residing beside DNA, they direct how, when, and which genes switch on in response to the environment throughout one's life. In the womb, epi-marks protect boys from underexposure and girls from overexposure to testosterone.

These switches are not typically hereditary, but, sometimes, they get passed on. In such cases, girls inherit the marks from their fathers and become masculine, while boys receive from their mothers and become feminine.

Homosexuality may indirectly benefit other members of the family, like increased fertility in women.

Other scientists wonder if homosexuality serves any purpose at all. Perhaps it rides piggyback on another beneficial adaptation that gets selected again and again, and homosexuality gets inadvertently chosen, too.

There probably is no single explanation for a behaviour found in so many different creatures.

Perhaps it is a result of gender shortage for some, male bonding, and genetic side-effects in others.

Among dogs, not all same-sex mountings are sexual but a show of dominance.

Most of our attempts to answer the paradox of homosexuality focus on the barrenness of same-sex. But many sexual acts are non-reproductive. Since sex also gives pleasure, to that end, homosexuality is no different from heterosexuality. Perhaps that's all there is to it.

Brains and Smarts

Are dogs more intelligent than cats? An online article stated dogs had bigger brains and were therefore more intelligent than cats.

In the past 20,000 years of our shared history, dogs have gone from being our hunting partners and livestock herders to participating in search and rescue teams, and law enforcement, acting as lifeguards, and assisting people with disabilities. Cats, however, have remained mere rodent catchers for 5,000 years.

Having known both cats and dogs, I was tempted to agree with the article's conclusion. But I wasn't convinced by the 'big brain, more intelligence' theory, since I'd have to concede that Rom was smarter than me.

In 1836, German anatomist Friedrich Tiedemann was the first to suggest that humans with bigger brains were more intelligent than others. 19th-century anthropologists obsessively measured human brains of every race they could. After World War II, the whole theory smacked of racial prejudice.

Neanderthals had larger brains than modern humans. Men have larger brains than women. One would expect Einstein's brain to be larger than average human brains, but it is smaller. Yet, some scientists argue there is a general trend towards higher intelligence with increase in brain size. While argument rages over using brain size as an indicator of intelligence in humans, biologists apply the big brain rule to animals.

Dogs generally are larger than cats, and among mammals, big brains are needed to control large bodies. Elephants and blue whales have the largest brains. To what degree does a large brain reflect intelligence?

There was another assumption: social animals like dogs are smarter than solitary animals such as cats. According to the Social Brain Hypothesis proposed by evolutionary biologist Robin Dunbar, in 1998, primates have large brains because of their hectic social lives. When social primates forage together, they compete with one another but also cooperate so the group procures more food.

Selfish desires and altruistic interests call for problem-solving skills that require extra brain power.

The Social Brain Hypothesis works differently in other mammals. Monogamous species have larger brains than polygamous ones. Canids have large brains since their packs revolve around a breeding pair.

Lions form coalitions with other males and live with prides of lionesses. Except for lions, felines don't have an intense social life.

I wondered if lions were smarter than tigers. Although

solitary tigers and social lions have roughly similar body size, tigers' brains are larger by 16 per cent. Even tigresses from Bali, the smallest of the species, have a similar brain size to large South African lions. Lions' brains ought to be the largest, according to 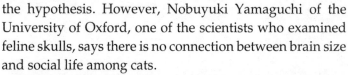 the hypothesis. However, Nobuyuki Yamaguchi of the University of Oxford, one of the scientists who examined feline skulls, says there is no connection between brain size and social life among cats.

How do we measure the intelligence of two animals with different brain sizes and social lives, especially if you can't give them an IQ test? Biologists commonly use the Encephalization Quotient (EQ) that takes body and brain sizes into account. The value is derived after deducting the estimated brain size needed to control the species' body mass from the actual brain size of the animal. For instance, on average, our brains are seven times larger than expected for our body size.

Humans come in many shapes, sizes, and weights—from short, stocky Nepalis to tall, lean Maasai. Body fat skews EQ, making trim people appear smarter than the obese. Therefore, EQ is considered inappropriate for humans.

Even among other mammals, EQ doesn't work across the spectrum. Small capuchin monkeys from South America have a greater EQ value than the more intelligent great apes. Until intelligence tests become foolproof, EQ continues to be used to measure animal intelligence. Dogs' EQ score is better than cats, and tigers are smarter than lions.

Perhaps house cats are smarter than they reveal, receiving the same rewards—our hearts and hearths—as high EQ, hard-working, social dogs, without having to do much.

The Round Ark

The Great Flood was imminent. To save man and animal kind, the Mesopotamian God Enki gave detailed instructions to Atra-hasis to build a gigantic ark. Contrary to our expectations, that ark wasn't a wooden ship with prow and stern like Noah's, but a round coracle.

While modern-day Iraq (Mesopotamia in ancient times) is said to have had coracles until the 1970s, we continue to use these simple boats to navigate the boulder-strewn, fast-flowing rivers of south India.

Our coracles are buoyant, bowl-shaped, buffalo-hide vessels supported by a bamboo basket framework and waterproofed with bitumen. In recent years, tarpaulin or nylon bags that once held fertilizer replaced hides. Only one paddle is needed to ply them. They are the ideal crafts to use, as wooden boats would be smashed to smithereens on the rocks.

Rom conducted a lot of his crocodile surveys on coracles. Without these crafts, he would have had to leg it. On the

Moyar river, Tamil Nadu, Kaliappan, his field assistant, manoeuvred the craft over eddies and away from sharp boulders. As the current swept them around a bend, they saw a herd of elephants slowly crossing the river ahead of them. Some leisurely drank, some sprayed water on their backs, while calves struggled to keep their trunk tips above the water.

Kaliappan tried to paddle toward the bank, but they were travelling too fast and the current was too strong. He tried to snag his paddle on rocks, but the smooth wood slipped. The men yelled to hurry up the animals, but the noise of water crashing over boulders drowned their voices. When it looked like the coracle was going to collide into this elephant phalanx, Rom grabbed an overhanging branch. Before the craft slipped away from under Rom, Kaliappan grabbed him and the branch. With the strong current tugging the coracle, the men barely managed to hang on until the last of the elephants clambered up the bank.

Rom would often lay low in a coracle and stealthily approach crocodiles without spooking them. One basking croc suddenly woke up to find a human almost nose to nose, taking its picture. When it dove under the coracle, the pointy scales on its back rubbed rat-a-tat against the bamboo ribs.

Coracles are versatile field vessels. At Sathanur dam, Rom and his team were crossing the reservoir at night. When they were in the middle of the vast artificial lake, a cold wind whipped up huge waves that swamped the craft. The driver paddled hard and reached the bank before a heavy downpour started. The men flipped the coracle over on the beach, propped it up with the paddle, and sheltered underneath, emerging dry the following morning.

Paddling this simple craft looks deceptively easy. For many winters, Rom went fishing for mahseer on the river Kaveri. We'd set out in a coracle with a gillie before dawn and spend the day on the river. When I grew bored of watching Rom fish, I wanted to try my hand at steering the coracle. But that stretch of the river was notorious for whirlpools and rapids. If I landed the coracle on one of the numerous rocks jutting out of the water, it could get punctured. Or worse, I could overturn it and land us all in the dangerous waters. Rom said he hadn't heard of a coracle flipping over; they are incredibly stable.

When I got my chance to steer one in calmer waters, I realized technique was crucial. With no keel or rudder, the boat spun around, and when I dug the paddle into the water, it spun the other way.

I wondered how Atra-hasis steered his 38,750-square foot coracle. The 20-feet-high walls would have been too high for an average man. Then I realized he didn't have to go anywhere. The coracle had to merely bob on the water with its precious cargo of animals and humans until the floodwaters receded: a job it was well-designed to perform.

The Adventures of a Crocodile Stud

The seven-foot-long mugger crocodile lived a solitary, tortured life at the Madras Aquarium on Marina Beach for at least fifteen years. His aquarium was just as long as he was. With no dry land on which he could haul out, he floated in water all the time. Not even a beam of sunlight sneaked in to warm his cold-blooded body. His keepers fed him a monotonous diet of fish. Any other creature would have gone mad under these conditions.

In the wild, the prospects of mugger crocodiles were dismal at that time. In 1974, Rom had just completed a countrywide survey and felt they had to be bred in captivity to improve their future prospects. He persuaded the director of the aquarium to give him the mugger croc.

At the Madras Snake Park, adjacent to Guindy Deer Park and the State Governor's residence—the Raj Bhavan—in the heart of the city, Rom examined the reptile. For having been submerged in water for such a long time, the crocodile surprisingly had no skin lesions. Although it's usually hard to divine what reptiles feel, it was clear he was delighted with his new outdoors enclosure. He thrashed the water with élan and strutted around his pen. He was named Periyor, meaning 'the respected one', in Tamil.

Before Periyor arrived, in March 1973, wild bonnet macaques slaked their thirst at the pond in his enclosure. But they somehow missed his showy display of possession, and one afternoon, trooped down to the water's edge as usual. Periyor charged out of the water and caught one. Living cooped up in an aquarium hadn't blunted his predatory instincts.

The breeding programme needed a female mugger. More than 200 kilometres south of Chennai, at Porto Novo, now called Parangipettai, the Snake Park's sea turtle survey team found a stunted, six-foot crocodile at a marine fisheries laboratory. The lab was glad to be rid of the animal, and she came to the Snake Park.

Rom put her in with Periyor and stood by, ready to break up any skirmish. Instead, these two mugger crocs that had never seen another of their kind for most of their lives started courting. Nobody at the Snake Park knew if mugger crocodiles would breed easily in captivity, nor did they know the mating or nesting season. This pleasant and auspicious start of a breeding programme was a surprise. Rom named her Nova.

When a keeper almost lost his leg to a suddenly aggressive Nova, Rom ordered her isolation and probed the soil until he found the nest. A debate ensued: let the eggs incubate naturally, or take them to an incubator. Eventually, he covered up the nest and let nature take its course.

A couple of months later, Nova swam around the pond with an arrangement of hatchlings on her head. Rom and his team felt as proud as new parents. Little did he know that twenty years later, he would have more than 2,000 mugger crocodiles weighing heavy on his head. But that's getting ahead of the story.

To extend the enclosure, Rom broke the wall and erected a makeshift chain-link fence in its place. These clumsy, stubby-legged creatures weren't likely to climb, were they?

In the morning, Periyor was missing. The tracks led from the chain-link fence, crossed under the Snake Park's barbed wire perimeter fence, and headed across the woods and a grassy meadow of Guindy Deer Park. Beyond lay the Raj Bhavan.

In the 1970s, the Governor's stately residence wasn't surrounded by a wall, but by a mere hedgerow. The ground was hard and the tracks were indistinct, but Rom was certain Periyor had made for the duck pond, within sight of the august mansion. Every morning, Governor K.K. Shah went for a brisk walk, and Rom hoped he hadn't seen the runaway crocodile yet.

Rom didn't waste any more time following the tracks. He rushed back to the office and was making arrangements to catch Periyor when the forest department called. The croc had been sighted at the duck pond, and the Governor had issued orders to shoot it on sight.

Rom entrusted his assistants, Rajamani, Motorcycle Mani, and Gundu Mani, with the job of putting together a catching team and gathering up ropes, while he rushed to the Raj Bhavan to meet the Governor. He explained Periyor was a tame crocodile and no danger to anyone. On Rom's assurance that he would catch the animal, the Governor rescinded his order.

Periyor gave the catching team the runaround in the half-acre pond. His head would pop up on one side of the pond, and when the men rushed over, he'd submerge. Hours passed as the team waited for the crocodile to resurface. Periyor may have had a calm temperament, but he displayed all the cunningness of a hunted animal. Perhaps just the tip of his snout came up for air without creating a ripple. If Periyor couldn't be seen, how was Rom to noose him?

Someone suggested isolating the croc to one side of the pond. And on the wise guy's suggestion, they lined up a row of scarecrows dressed in football jerseys, but the croc wasn't intimidated. Rom baited a trap with chicken guts, but wily Periyor evaded capture and ate the bait. Within a couple of days, the catching operation became a public spectacle.

Back then, Raj Bhavan didn't have the security we now take for granted. People walked in from the road to watch the futile catching attempts. Popcorn and peanut sellers set up stands. Rom grew increasingly embarrassed by his own ineptitude, and the Governor was becoming impatient. Rom needed to somehow sweep across the breadth of the pond in one fell swoop.

Eventually, he came up with a plan. He sought a trawl and some sturdy trainees from a fisheries' training institute. The 40-feet-long and 20-feet-wide net was heavy. With long ropes tied to the ends, twenty muscular men trawled the pond. As the net was being hauled up, everyone expected a croc to come out, thrashing and snapping. Instead, decades of rotting mesquite thorns surfaced, and a dozen turtles scrambled around. The bottom of the net was inert and heavy with debris. Had the croc given them a miss again?

Thorns scratched the disappointed men as they removed the turtles. When the net was fully opened, a slush-disguised Periyor charged forward, snapping his jaws. Relieved that the public spectacle was over, Rom hauled him back to the Snake Park and patched up the enclosure wall with concrete.

Two years later, Periyor and Nova moved to a spacious enclosure at the Madras Crocodile Bank on the coast. At ten feet, he was the biggest croc and the star attraction, and he lorded over a harem of female muggers. The stud male was also remarkably light-coloured for the species, which led to many jokes of him being a white foreigner like Rom.

Mugger crocs dig tunnels during the dry season. Digging is easy in the sandy soil, and if left alone, crocs could breach the foundations of the enclosure walls. Before the facility opened to the public each morning, keepers at the Croc Bank filled these tunnels to prevent crocs making their escape.

One summer morning, in 1983, Periyor went missing. Had he escaped once again? The workers searched the premises but found nothing, not even tracks.

Two days later, keepers discovered him. He had dug a deep tunnel, and the roof had collapsed on him. Since the mouth of the tunnel had also collapsed, no one had known of its existence. The weight of the sand had killed him.

Rom was in distant Papua New Guinea when he heard the sad news. The easy-going, calm-natured animal had a special place in Rom's heart; Periyor was his first crocodile.

The croc that survived spirit-crushing solitude for 15 years with equanimity, and a Governor's threat, too, sired hundreds of babies in his decade-long career as a crocodilian stud.

Love in the Time of Danger

I didn't realize the implications of Rom's endeavour to breed king cobras in captivity until eight adult snakes arrived from various zoos in 1995. He already had several venomous snakes of other species, and I mistakenly assumed king cobras would merely add to the menagerie.

These snakes averaged 10 feet in length, and the largest was a hefty 12-footer. Each needed a 100-square foot room of its own. The rooms were separated by four-foot-high brick walls topped with welded wire mesh.

Rom spent a couple of hours every day feeding or examining them. Or, the rooms needed cleaning. Even if the snakes didn't need attention, he made sure they got it. I, too, liked the creatures, but his fervour was unmatched. Only then did I realize Rom was besotted with king cobras.

I was intimidated by the snakes' size and the enormous venom glands bulging under their cheeks. I was edgy whenever he was with them, worried he might get bitten.

Rom is allergic to horse serum, which makes the life-saving antivenom as dangerous as venom.

I had nightmares of a king cobra clamping its jaws on him and not letting go, and often woke us up by shouting in my sleep.

I would have been happier if he didn't have anything to do with these dangerous snakes. But he was already an expert on reptiles by the time we met, and it seemed presumptuous I should enter his life and dictate conditions.

Rom's efforts were successful and four female king cobras grew heavy with eggs. Since this is the only species of snake to build a nest, we were all curious to see how a limbless creature did it. I had my cameras ready and batteries fully charged for the event.

It was evening when one of the egg-laden female king cobras became restless. Ceaselessly, she climbed up tree branches in her enclosure and burrowed under the thick pile of leaf litter lying on the ground that Rom had given her as nesting material.

Rom asked his assistants to put her neighbours on each side into their hide boxes, so I could film the nesting through the hatches he cut in the welded mesh walls. Each hide box had a hole on the side through which the snake could enter. All the assistants had to do was nudge them, and when they slid into the safety of their boxes, shove the doors shut.

Once I received the all-clear, I spread my gear on top of a box and began filming. The female king cobra gathered clumps of leaves in her coils and dropped them at the nest site. Hours later, when she had a high mound, she laid her eggs, covered them up, and lay exhausted on top of her nest. Although I had done little more than take pictures, I, too, was dog-tired. My watch displayed 3 a.m.

I was packing my gear while stifling a yawn, when I noticed a movement. The door of the hide box was open, and a massive king cobra's head was just a couple of inches away from my bare feet. Someone had forgotten to close the hatch.

I stood paralyzed. If I moved, would he latch on to my foot? Was this real or a nightmare? Then I snapped out of it and hurried out of the room. Closing the door, I told Rom of the open hide box. My brain dimly registered his anger at this security lapse.

I wondered why the 12-foot snake hadn't bitten me. Why had he sat complacently for nine hours, just watching me trampling across his room? He had numerous opportunities to bite me through the night. That gaping exit opened the doors of my perception of king cobras.

For the first time in his life, Rom feared for someone he loved. With my life and limb spared, I felt a surfeit of affection for king cobras. We had swapped emotions.

Just Another Croc in the Wall

Their long, stout bodies and short, stubby legs make crocodiles look ungainly. Apparently, only people who study, live, or work with them know that these reptiles can climb well. A recently published account highlighting how widespread this behaviour is among croc species received wide publicity.

Young crocs of many species routinely climb trees. In forests and mangroves, where no dry beach is available, these creatures have little option but to scale logs and trees to bask. Not only can they scramble up broad, sloping branches, but also thin, vertical ones that requires agility.

In captivity, crocodiles put their climbing skills to good use. An adult dwarf croc escaped from its enclosure in Bristol Zoo by crawling up a tree. And there's Periyor who scaled a 1.8 metre-high chain-link fence and escaped.

Some species like Australian freshwater crocs are better climbers than others such as saltwater crocs. Gharials, the most aquatic of all crocodilians, are probably the most inept climbers; they can't even walk a few paces. Generally, a crocodile's size determines how well it can scramble up. As the croc grows larger, the forelegs become progressively incapable of supporting its weight.

Crocs don't only climb trees and chain-link fences. They also scale steep, almost vertical, sandbanks. In our experience, the champions of crocodilian agility are muggers.

During a summer in Yala National Park, Sri Lanka, when most water bodies were dry, we found scats of adult muggers beside deep rainwater pools on top of steep, rocky outcrops, 15 metres above ground. But Rom had witnessed even better climbing feats.

Rom did the first survey of crocodiles at Gir, Gujarat, in 1975, a drought year. While spot-lighting for the reptiles in a drying artificial lake in Gir National Park, Rom mimicked the call of a distressed croc hatchling at night. He wanted to demonstrate to the foresters accompanying him how crocodile parents can be protective.

The foresters thought Rom was joking until a 2.5-metre mugger croc, plump from feasting on fish, emerged from the water. Rom's companions grinned in appreciation that a wild croc could be called like a puppy. But the croc was no tame creature.

She trundled purposefully out of the water, and the next thing the unsuspecting foresters saw was her head emerge over the three-metre-high edge. They stood frozen in shock. Only when she paused to get better purchase, did they recover their wits and beat a hasty retreat.

When permanent water is scarce, mugger crocs dig

deep tunnels in which they stay cool even when the outside temperatures are scorching. The 20-metre-high embankment of the 764-hectare Kamleshwar reservoir was riddled with tunnels all the way from the water's edge to the top.

Rom explored the lower tunnels and found nests near some of them. He couldn't climb up the embankment to investigate the tunnels located higher. He walked across the dry lake bed to the opposite bank where the slope was shallow and scrambled up. He circled back to the tunnel-riddled earthen wall, leaned over, and flashed a light into the topmost tunnel. The nose of a large three-metre male croc was no more than an arm's length away.

When Rom narrated this tale, I asked, 'Did the croc get into the tunnel when the water level was higher and become marooned when the water dried up?'

'There was a well-worn path leading down to the water,' he replied. 'So the croc was probably going down to the water for a drink every few days and climbing back into its tunnel.' After a pause, he added, 'These crocs were better at climbing than me.'

At night, Rom returned to spotlight for crocs from the opposite bank and found bright, reflective eyes glinting back at him from all the tunnels.

I wonder what would have happened if he had mimicked the distress calls of a baby croc.

The Magic Torch

I was terrified of *The Magic Tinderbox* story as a child. The tale's soldier-hero struck an enchanted match, and instead of a genie, three supernatural dogs appeared to do his bidding. The accompanying illustration of black, shaggy mutts with lips curled back into snarls and ghoulish greenish-white eyes sent shivers down my spine. One dog's eyes were saucer-sized, the second one's were the size of dinner plates, while the third had eyes as large as windmills. Had I known of eyeshine, I may not have been so petrified.

Animals active at night need to see in the dark. Their eyes have a reflective membrane, *tapetum lucidum*, meaning 'bright tapestry'. Light enters the dilated pupils and hits the back of the retina where the tapetum is usually located. The membrane bounces light back to the retina, enhancing the animal's night vision. It's this reflected eyeshine that we see blazing back at us.

At Madras Crocodile Bank, Rom showed me how to hold

the torch close to my eyes to see crocodile eyeshines. In one of the large enclosures, hundreds of bright, unblinking spots glowed in the dark as if planets on the night sky had fallen down. While driving through forest roads in Karnataka and Kerala, I saw the bright eyes of civets, deer, flying squirrels, gaurs, jackals, and dholes.

Frequently, all we see is a pair of bright eyes before the animal vanishes into darkness. Some wildlife specialists claim they can identify the creature just from the colour of eyeshine. Different substances make up the tapetum that may reflect specific colours. In crocodiles, the membrane's guanine crystals reflect red, cats have riboflavin rods that glow greenish-yellow, while cows and sheep have fibrous collagen that makes their eyes gleam blue. Dogs' tapetum is made of zinc cysteine, and my dogs' eyes reflect blue, green, white, red, or yellow.

Tapetum is iridescent, and the colour varies with the animal's position. That's why I'm not convinced you can identify animals by eyeshine colour alone. Colour and intensity may also depend on whether the torch has halogen or LED bulb.

Ishan Agarwal of the Centre for Ecological Sciences,

Bangalore, taught us how to search for small, pretty geckos that are well-camouflaged in the leaf litter. The trick is to use a dull, incandescent torch that emits yellow light.

In Sri Lanka, Rom and I stayed in a rest house overlooking the large pond of Katagamuwa, Yala National Park. We decided to sleep in the mosquito net-draped beds on the verandah as it was too stuffy inside the room. The ranger accompanying us narrated an incident of how a leopard had mauled someone sleeping in the open.

After nightfall, while Rom spotlit the pond for crocodiles, I scanned the forest for leopards. While he chanted quietly under his breath, '99, 100, 101,' my beam of light picked up little more than spiders that have surprisingly bright eyeshine for their size.

We fell asleep listening to the sounds of the forest: dry leaves rattling in the wind, the distant trumpeting of elephants, a rodent or civet scurrying around the roof, the monotonous call of a nightjar, and the sudden startling lapwing scream, *'Didyoudoit ... didyoudoit.'*

I woke up in the middle of the night to take a swig of water and scanned the forest with a torch. The brightest pair of eyes, the aura of light as big as saucers, stared back at me. I roused Rom, all my dormant childhood fears making my hair stand on end. His powerful spotlight revealed a leopard. A moment later, the cat disappeared among the trees.

Five years later, a leopard moved into our farm. Every night, I scan the perimeter with a torch, while our dogs do their last business of the day in the garden. I feel like that soldier when I switch on the torch. Would the light summon ole saucer eyes?

Ironically, while tapetum allows creatures to see better in darkness, its bright beacon-like reflection gives the animals away.

A Rock Symphony

I visited the rock of Mehrangarh on the inauguration of Rao Jodha Desert Park in February 2012, and it took my breath away. The park was 70 hectares of solid stone—hard, volcanic, pinkish rhyolite found in only one other location in Asia: in eastern China.

I could see no soil, but there were plants aplenty—glorious stands of green, leafless spurge covered with bright red blossoms, greyish-green clumps of seddera, latex-filled green stems of rambling milkweed, and fuzzy heads of young gum arabic trees. They had the uncanny skill of sending roots deep into fissures and finding a lick of moisture.

But what of the shallow-rooted grasses whose drying seed heads were ablaze with the warm colours of the setting sun? They lived abbreviated lives of fast-burning candles—germinating, flowering, and seeding after the scant, brief monsoon.

The rock wasn't always bursting with native life. In

fact, most of these herbs, shrubs, and trees had been planted in a restoration effort by Pradip Krishen, Delhi's tree man.

From almost anywhere in the rocky park, I could see the towering six-century-old Mehrangarh Fort, the Citadel of the Sun. It rose sharp-angled and steep-walled out of the rocky hill overlooking the city of Jodhpur. The ramparts were cannonball-proof. The warren of staircases, audience halls, and private rooms of royalty long since dead was maze-like.

In 1900, Rudyard Kipling described it as 'The work of angels, fairies and giants...built by Titans and coloured by the morning sun...he who walks through it loses sense of being among buildings. It is as though he walked through mountain gorges.'

Pradip introduced me to the descendants of some of these 'angels, fairies and giants'. They possessed neither angelic wings nor the petiteness of fairies. None was taller than 5 feet 6 inches. The turbaned Khandwalias with ornament-studded ears and large, calloused hands are a hereditary community of specialist rock miners.

Before the park could be planted with native flora, Pradip had to contend with a nightmare. The whole rocky expanse had been taken over by Prosopis, a Mexican invasive. If any native plant was to survive, the Latinos had to go. The only way to be rid of them was by uprooting their roots embedded in rock. After several unsuccessful attempts, a desperate Pradip, who's as tenacious as the Prosopis he sought to eradicate, enlisted the Khandwalias' help.

Just as desert plants sought fissures, these people knew how to find and exploit fault lines deep inside the rock.

Like drummers tuning their instruments, the skilled artisans tapped the rhyolite around a tree with a mallet and listened to the tone, resonance, and pitch. Once they determined where the weakness lay, they knew how to attack rock and root.

In many places on the rocky hill, hard rhyolite is topped by soft sandstone. The Khandwalias' ancestors probably used the same rapping technique to hew blocks of sandstone for constructing the fort.

Although work began on a hot summer day in May 1459, the castle reached its splendour two centuries later. In more recent times, it fell into disrepair. The current custodian, Gaj Singh II, created the Mehrangarh Museum Trust in the 1970s to restore the 11-hectare stone castle. The fine architectural shell of the Mehrangarh fort, one of the best preserved in the country, harks back to the lifestyle of a historical past.

To the royal family of Jodhpur, the dense rock offered the best defence in preceding centuries; to the Khandwalias, the resonating rock sang its deepest secrets; and to Pradip, the cracked rock sustained delicate desert plants.

Although Rao Jodha Park is a contemporary living ecosystem, home to civets, boar, hares, and birds such as

nightjars, it recalls an even more ancient time—one that precedes the fort.

The past rubs shoulders with the present, architectural heritage sits alongside the ecological, and human valour flanks botanical vigour on the rock of Jodhpur.

All You Need is Magic

Rom met Jack Cox Jr. in Papua New Guinea when the Food and Agriculture Organization hired them to work on a crocodile ranching project. Rom went from river to river surveying crocodiles, while Jack set to work convincing tribesmen along the river Sepik to stop hunting adult crocodiles.

Each clan had a totem animal, and it was taboo for members to harm or eat that species. Members of the crocodile clan thought of the reptiles as their siblings, and they didn't need to be convinced. But the majority belonged to other clans such as cassowary, praying mantis, and hornbill, and tribal custom didn't prevent them from hunting crocodiles.

Changing people's minds is tricky business. In West Bengal, I've futilely argued the role of elephants in the ecosystem and left villagers unmoved. But when I mentioned the centuries-old tradition of worshipping the elephant-headed god Ganesh, they immediately made an emotional connection. Even though scientific facts sound perfectly logical, people tend to cling to tradition and religious practice.

Not surprisingly, conservation was a tough sell for Jack, especially since customary law didn't prohibit hunting crocodiles. By living in a remote village for several months and helping villagers in their daily chores, Jack eventually gained their trust and succeeded in getting most of them to stop hunting crocs.

As always, there was one troublesome character. A hunter continued killing adult female crocodiles by setting hooks and nets at nests. No matter how hard Jack tried, he couldn't change the man's mind.

Soon after a public argument with Jack, the drunken hunter gunned his motorboat down the river. He fell overboard and was flailing when the driverless boat made a wide circle and hit him. He was knocked unconscious and drowned.

Villagers were convinced Jack had cast a spell on the recalcitrant hunter and looked upon him with fear and respect. Much to Jack's discomfort, the story of his purported witchcraft travelled up and down the river. Thenceforth, his word was law.

Jack later moved to Irian Jaya (now called West Papua) to head a similar crocodile project, relieved to start afresh in a new place with no mumbo-jumbo clinging to him. Until another incident occurred.

He drove a colleague down the ghat road from Sentani airport to Jayapura one rainy night. A lorry coming from Jayapura took a bend too fast, and Jack swerved to the verge to avoid a collision. Softened by rain, the shoulder gave way.

The Jeep tumbled down the 1000-foot drop. The passenger door flew open as the vehicle bounced off the slope, and Jack's colleague, who wasn't wearing his seat belt, fell out. The Jeep crashed through the roof of a hut in a shantytown on the edge of Jayapura, at the base of the hill.

Miraculously, the vehicle landed on its tyres. With the seat belt holding him in place, a shaken Jack sat upright, gripping the steering wheel tightly. When he gathered his wits and looked around, he saw a sleeping baby gently swinging in a hammock a couple of yards away. Jack felt himself all over; there were no broken bones, but he was severely bruised.

His colleague was in bad shape.

When rescuers found him, he had blood oozing out of his ears and suffered multiple fractures.

It seemed incredible that anyone could survive the spectacular fall with no major injuries. Then there was the baby, unhurt and still asleep. To the local dwellers, it could only be magic, and Jack was clearly not a man to be crossed.

Jack went to great lengths to explain how the seat belt may have saved him, but no one believed him. Rom urged him, 'Use your reputation for croc conservation.' But Jack demurred. He just wanted to be an ordinary bloke fighting an uphill battle against all the odds. And he didn't want any supernatural shortcuts.

It's a tricky business changing people's minds.

Jack Cox died of cerebral malaria on 22 June 2010.

In Search of a Leatherback

Five of us headed north from camp on West Bay, Little Andaman. The full moon shone brightly on the beach, and we didn't need torches to light our way. No ships twinkled on the horizon, nor was there any evidence of humanity. We crossed old turtle tracks eroded by the wind.

Since 2010, a consortium of research organizations led by Kartik Shanker and Naveen Namboothri, Indian Institute of Science, Bangalore, had tagged seven leatherbacks on this beach. We were looking to wire up the eighth turtle with a transmitter.

If we came upon one, there would be no time to lose. While the turtle laid eighty to 100 eggs, the researchers would drill a hole through the central bony ridge on her back and tie a satellite transmitter with plastic-coated wire. Tough luck if she finished laying her eggs before the researchers were done. There was no way to restrain a behemoth weighing up to 900 kilograms.

As exciting as the opportunity was, my back was killing

me, and I couldn't walk any farther. I considered crashing out on the sand right there, but there were saltwater crocodiles about. I hobbled back to camp and curled up in my sleeping bag, breathing the strong-smelling vapours of muscle relaxant.

Waves crashed ashore in a loud *boom*, numerous crabs scratched around the tent, and in the forest, a Verreaux's gecko barked rhythmically.

I lay awake, thinking of the record-setting globetrotters. Leatherbacks were the largest turtles in the world; they dove down to 1,200 metres, more than any other reptile; they migrated the farthest, from the tropics to subarctic waters; and they ate a monotonous diet of jellyfish. Instead of a hard, smooth shell, hard rubber-like thick skin stretched over seven ridges, running lengthwise down their backs.

One turtle tagged on West Bay reached Timor, 7,312 kilometres away, in 179 days. Another leatherback swam south of Maldives, hung around Diego Garcia for a few days before heading for Seychelles, a distance of 6,998 kilometres, in 183 days. Two others passed Cocos (Keeling) Islands. Final destinations of these turtles remain unknown, as the radio devices malfunctioned.

A leatherback tagged in Papua New Guinea by another group of researchers crossed the Pacific and reached northern US. A couple of months later, she popped down to Hawaii, for a sojourn in tropical waters for the next five months.

When Kartik had briefed us on the project's results, I asked, 'What does this scattering across the oceans mean?'

'Sea turtle hatchlings spend most of their time circling oceans on large gyres and currents,' he answered. 'At some point in their development, they find good feeding grounds, and when they become adults, return to their natal shores to nest. They probably then return to those same feeding grounds because they don't know any others.'

I woke up when the team returned at 2.30 a.m. I knew from their tired but happy faces that they had tagged a turtle. They narrated how it happened. They had sat down to rest awhile. When it was time to continue walking, Meera, Kartik's partner, stood up and stretched, wistfully saying, 'Wouldn't it be nice if a turtle came up and nested right here?'

There in the surf, at that very moment, she saw a leatherback waiting for the coast to clear. They kept a low profile until the turtle heaved herself on to the shore and began digging a nest hole. If only I had been able to walk an hour longer, I, too, might have seen the turtle.

For the next two nights, I walked a stretch of the 7-kilometre beach with others, but no turtle came ashore.

Six months later, that turtle was off the coast of Dampier Peninsula, north-western Australia.

One of these winters, with the same certainty as

leatherbacks navigate across the oceans, I'm taking my now-healed back to that little speck of an arrowhead-shaped island in the Andaman Sea.

Why are Some Snakes Venomous?

'Both ratsnakes and Russell's vipers eat the same thing: rats. But why is one species venomous and the other not?' asked 11-year-old Abhinav.

A group of children and adults, who had landscaped a waterhole on the farm, were about to leave, when the sharp, young lad posed this question. I don't think Rom and my answers were adequate in the limited time, so here is a more elaborate explanation.

Overpowering prey is a challenge for limbless creatures. Some species, like Russell's viper, inject venom; some others opt for an alternative non-chemical method. Ratsnakes, for instance, grab and push their prey against the ground, while pythons use their brawn to squeeze their quarry to death. But snakes can't be neatly divided into venomous and non-venomous categories.

Rom and I watched a bullfrog whose head was caught in the vice-like jaws of a slender vine snake. Although the amphibian seemed too big for the snake, it wasn't strong enough to escape. Could the snake's mild venom kill the large frog? If it did, could the serpent swallow its quarry?

An hour later, the frog became sluggish as a bright yellow spot slowly grew larger on its head. When the amphibian went limp, the snake struggled to swallow it. We grew frustrated watching its attempts to wrap its pointed, narrow mouth around the frog's head. Perhaps tired or realizing the futility of the effort, it dropped the frog and slithered into the bushes. We examined the dead amphibian and concluded the yellow spot may have been caused by the vine snake's venom.

When a vine snake latched on to Rom's middle finger, he patiently pried it off with a pen even as it chewed on him. If he yanked his hand away, its teeth would break and squeezing out each tooth is a painful business. His finger swelled up and itched for twenty-four hours. Since their bites aren't fatal to humans, these snakes are called 'mildly venomous'. But to their quarry, they can be lethal.

Even species listed as non-venomous aren't completely devoid of venom. The common sand boa, for instance, produces secretions particularly toxic to birds. So the species doesn't hedge its bets; it constricts its prey and injects venom for good measure.

Do vipers need venom potent enough to kill hundreds of rats with just one drop? After all, they eat only one or two at a time.

While predators try their darnedest to kill most efficiently, their prey use any trick to avoid becoming a meal, such as developing immunity to venom. For instance, Californian ground squirrels are resistant to Northern Pacific rattlesnake venom. Venomous snakes need to maintain their edge by evolving venom toxic enough to override immunity. We don't know if any of our Indian rodents use this trick.

Competition with prey is not the only thing driving snakes to evolve more and more toxic venom. Snakes also struggle to avoid becoming prey themselves.

Some snake predators have partial immunity to venom. Famously, mongooses are highly resistant to cobra venom, and with their speed and agility, kill snakes with impunity. It would be the death of cobras as a species if they didn't evolve more toxic venom to immobilize mongooses.

Venom has another important role. It is an extreme meat tenderizer; specific enzymes disintegrate the innards of prey. Normally, a reptile depends on the sun's warm rays to aid digestion. Venomous snakes have an advantage: enzymes in venom digest the meal from the inside before it rots in their guts. These same enzymes cause considerable tissue damage in human snakebite victims.

But I wonder if we cannot use venom in our favour. In remote parts of India, local hospitality often involves leather-tough meat. I chew and chew until my jaws ache. If I spit it out or refuse, our hosts would be offended. Eventually, I swallow like a python stuffing a deer down its throat and hope I don't choke.

If only I had venom.

Is Nature Photography Art?

Ganesh H. Shankar suspected the audience would think he was mad. With that preamble, the software engineer described the seventeen-year passion for his hobby to a room full of photographers.

Like many attending the wildlife photography festival, Nature inFocus, Bangalore, Ganesh set off every weekend with his photographic artillery to stalk wildlife. A perfectly framed image of an owl stared at us from the screen, and he pointed out that every barb of every feather was in sharp focus. If only I could take pictures like that.

Ganesh remembered debating the merits of one lens versus another, one brand with another, and focussing on the technical aspects of photography. Many photographers, gathered to listen to his talk, would have recognized themselves in his description of himself. Left-brain photography, Ganesh called that period. He may have been self-deprecating, but a friend whispered, 'He's making fun of all of us.' I wondered what Ganesh was going to say next.

'I caught a disease called creativity,' he said. Photographs of birds and mammals gave way to smaller creatures. A submerged frog's bug-eyes peered at a water drop suspended a couple of millimetres above the water surface. In another photograph, he used long exposure to capture the flight of a moth. Playfully, he called it right-brain photography.

'Was photographing nature merely chronicling beauty?' he asked. No one in the audience coughed, sneezed, or murmured.

Could nature photography be an art form? Ganesh turned to Leo Tolstoy for answers. The writer had famously declared beauty was not necessary in a work of art, but it must convey feeling. The stronger the emotion it expresses, the better the art. But how does a nature photographer express himself when we can't read his animal subjects' emotions?

Ganesh looked at other art forms—theatre, music, movies, and dance. Since they all dealt with the human condition, it was easy for artists to communicate their feelings. The only art form that had some relevance to

his quandary was instrumental music. If Raga Bhairav in Hindustani music can evoke daybreak, surely he could do something similar with photographs.

Ganesh began experimenting with light, shape, and form. Deliberately, he misaligned his lens, and sometimes even tilted it at an angle from the camera. His photographs from this phase looked like abstract paintings. Ganesh ended his talk with, 'I don't know where I'm going.'

Later that evening, I asked him to explain the similarities he saw between nature photography and instrumental music.

'Ragas are soothing when there aren't many variations, when there is a gradual movement of notes,' he replied. 'Evening ragas extract less energy from the listener compared to morning or noon ragas. Sad music also cannot have strident tempo. So musicians induce mood with tempo, arrangement of notes, and rhythm. Light and sound are scientifically similar; both are waves. I wonder … can you use light of different intensities to create a sad or joyful mood? Higher intensity light may be joyful and energetic, while mid-tones with few variations may denote sadness.' This is an idea cinema already uses.

A photograph of a lone hunched vulture perched atop a bare tree, reminiscent of Chinese ink painting, is captioned *Defeated*. A stooped human may look crushed, but that's a healthy vulture in repose. Is it necessary for an artist to remain true to the subject's emotion? Did we ever wonder what the model posing for Leonardo da Vinci felt?

An artist evokes a subjective reality, i.e., his or her own experience. When the audience responds to the creation, it becomes art, says Tolstoy.

Ganesh isn't the first to use the idiom of nature to create art. He follows in the tradition of landscape and still-life painters like John Constable and Vincent van Gogh.

Creating a work of art does indeed need a flash of madness.

The Case of the Dwarf-tiger

In the many years of traipsing through Kerala, the fishing cat didn't figure in conversations with our jungle-trekking companions. No one I knew had ever seen it. Recently, when our friend Manori Gunawardena in Sri Lanka sent pictures of an orphaned kitten she was rearing, I wondered why the species was absent from South India.

At first glance, it seems to belong to wetlands and mangroves along the coast, from northern Andhra Pradesh, Orissa, Bengal, Bangladesh, and into Southeast Asia. But it is also found far inland in Rajasthan's Ranthambore and Bharatpur, and along the foothills of the Himalayas. If it can be found in isolated pockets in a desert state, why not in the verdant West coast? Besides, the species must need a launching pad somewhere in South India to colonize Sri Lanka.

In 1874, zoologist Thomas Jerdon, who served as a civil surgeon in Thalassery, North Kerala, wrote the comprehensive *The Mammals of India*. He reported the tiger cat, as he called the feisty species, was, 'tolerably common in Travancore and Ceylon, extending up the Malabar coast as far as Mangalore.'

In November 1903, herpetologist Capt. Frank Wall found a kitten while out snipe hunting near Kannur, North Kerala. Stanley Prater, the author of the 1948 treatise *The Book of Indian Animals*, also reported a kitten from the same area.

Wildlife enthusiast Roopak Gangadharan says an elderly fisherman in the backwaters of the region identified the species as *kuri-nari*, meaning 'dwarf tiger'. What an appropriate name for a hefty, feisty cat!

Did the West coast habitat change more than the species could tolerate? In 2011, Tiasa Adhya, a student of wildlife biology at National Centre for Biological Sciences, Bangalore, surveyed the highly human populated districts of Howrah and Hooghly around Kolkata. In her report, she noted dense stands of native reeds were vital for the species to survive.

But how does one explain the fishing cat's adaptability elsewhere? In April 2014, one fell into a village well on the banks of the heavily polluted river Yamuna, not far downstream from Delhi. In Sri Lanka, it prowls the outskirts of Colombo city and tea estates in the hilly heart of the island.

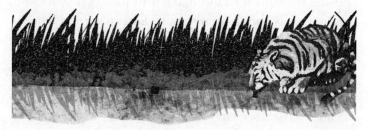

Did a shortage of prey in Kerala do the cat in? That's unlikely, as it lives on fish and molluscs, grabs waterfowl by their legs by swimming underwater, and around villages, it is notorious for taking poultry and goats.

Jerdon quoted a Mr Baker from Malabar: 'It often kills pariah dogs, and that he has known instances of slave children (infants) being taken from their huts by this cat.' In Colombo, where waterways are polluted and fish may be hard to find, it takes stray dogs and cats.

Perhaps the problem wasn't habitat or prey, but people's dislike of the species. Tiasa noted Bengali villagers set out poison and traps for livestock-taking cats. It's possible such hounding could have led to its local extinction from Kerala. There is one problem with this theory: there is no evidence.

However, there's another possibility: the cat never inhabited the West coast, even though the landscape seems ideal.

Ignoring Jerdon and Wall's observations, zoologist Reginald Innes Pocock failed to mention Kerala as fishing cat territory. He edited the second edition of *The Fauna of British India: Mammalia*, in 1939, without setting foot in India.

If the fishing cat didn't make it to the West coast, did it colonize Sri Lanka from the dry East coast? Evidence it lived in arid Tamil Nadu is scarcer still.

Shomita Mukherjee, a biologist working on cats, hypothesizes that the higher salinity of the Arabian Sea may account for the absence of the species along the Malabar coast. If coastal waters are saline, what prevents the fishing cat from prowling inland through the hills of the Western Ghats, as it does in the Sri Lankan highlands?

We are none the wiser as we have no hide nor scat nor photo of the species from Kerala. All we have is an enigmatic name: kuri-nari.

Bringing Up a Snake Freak

What would you do if your five-year-old son or daughter brought a live snake home? Would you say, 'Here's a container to keep it'? Or would you throw a fit and admonish the child?

When five-year-old Rom proudly brought a live milksnake, Doris, his mother, gave him a container for it.

A few months earlier, he had brought a dead snake to his home in Hoosick, a village in northern New York state. Gail, his nine-year-old sister, was horrified.

'Why did you kill the poor thing?' she demanded.

Taken aback, he explained, 'I didn't kill it. I found it dead in a garden down the street. Someone drove a lawn mower over it.'

Gail's initial reaction made a lasting impression on Rom. When he brought the milksnake home, the family approved. And the die was cast.

Decades later, I asked Doris if she hadn't been worried for her son's safety.

'I knew there were no venomous snakes in Hoosick, so I wasn't worried,' she replied.

That was a time when the reptiles, venomous or non-venomous, hadn't gained acceptance. Doris wasn't like any other mom in Hoosick village. She encouraged her son's peculiar interest, buying him *Boy's Book of Snakes* and taking him to the Museum of Natural History in New York City.

Out in the country, Rom went fishing in the Hoosack river with other village kids and observed tadpoles, turtles, insects, and birds.

A couple of years later, the family moved to a nation the West saw as the fabled land of snakes and snake charmers: India. He didn't plunge into the countryside headfirst, looking for his favourite animals; he was limited by the urban landscape of Bombay. So he did the next best thing: befriend snake charmers so he could play with their non-venomous animals, while paying no attention to their nonsensical beliefs about snakes.

When Rom was ten, he was packed off to boarding school in Kodaikanal. In the following years, he spent a lot of his free time in the surrounding forests.

On one such camping trip with a group of classmates, Rom saw a snake swimming across a pool and scooped it up with a butterfly net. To everyone's surprise, it turned out to be a Russell's viper. Nobody knew the species lived in these high altitudes. This was his first capture of a hot 'un, as venomous snakes are known in herp circles. He dumped it into his tin lunch box and took it to the school's biology lab.

The biology teacher was another adult who encouraged Rom's potentially perilous avocation, but he sensibly suggested the viper might be more dangerous than they could handle. Rom let the snake go.

But the teacher allowed him to keep less-venomous pit vipers in the lab. Can you imagine any teacher allowing a teenager to keep such dangerous animals in school today?

As a high school student, Rom frequented the Shenbaganur museum below Kodai. The helpful Jesuit priests, who were also naturalists, pulled out all their snake specimens for him. His eyes grew big when he saw a massive preserved king cobra head, and the curator said the snake had been killed nearby. Rom hadn't realized king cobras were found in the Palnis. My eyes grew big when he recounted that the priests had encouraged him to look for king cobras every weekend. Did they really mean it? Or were they trying to be rid of the teenager, certain he wouldn't find a king cobra?

What were these adults thinking, encouraging a snake-besotted lad? There were so many opportunities for things to take a bad turn. Doris probably didn't know of Rom's escapades in Kodai. In later years, she was so proud of him, she said she had full confidence in his abilities. She was the most important person to shape his career.

I asked Rom how his career would have turned out had Doris not been encouraging in his childhood.

'I'd have probably been a fisherman,' Rom replied.

Did Crocodile Hunters Use Babies as Bait in India?

The baby screamed in protest. She crawled as far as the rope tied around her waist allowed. Her screams rose above the gentle murmurs of the river. A large scaly beast emerged quietly from the water and lumbered towards the child.

A loud explosion rent the air, stopping the crocodile in its tracks and silencing the baby's cries. The crocodile thrashed for a few seconds before dying. A white hunter emerged from behind a bush and walked over to the dead crocodile. His assistant untied the toddler and she started bawling her head off.

Back in the village, the hunter, a former officer of the British army, paid the child's mother the equivalent of 6 cents. The baby proved to be his most successful crocodile bait, getting him more than 100 crocodiles in this manner.

'She was a real siren in luring the big reptiles to their

fate, and I was sorry to see her grow and get too big for bait and have to give her up,' wrote the hunter. This account of hunting crocodiles in India is based on his letter published on 1 July 1894 in the New York-based newspaper *The Sun*.

He claimed all a hunter had to do was announce his intention to go hunting for crocodiles and mothers flocked to him, offering their babies as bait. 'Some mothers required a guarantee that their offspring should be returned safe and sound, but the most of them exacted no such agreement. The babies were brought back alright as a rule, but once in a while some sportsman was a trifle slow with his rifle, or made a bad shot, and the crocodile got away with the bait, but that didn't happen often.'

Babies that cried loudly were the best bait. 'I've seen half a dozen crocodiles come hurrying from as many different parts of the river toward a baby five minutes after it was set,' he wrote. A rifle shot would kill one and send the rest diving into the water. But these hunters were apparently not heartless. 'A considerate sportsman, though, would not work his baby more than fifteen minutes at a time. Then he will have his native servant soothe it and refresh it from a nursing bottle, which is part of a crocodile hunter's equipment.'

India was not an exception. If such news reports are to be believed, hunters' use of human babies appears to have been prevalent in Sri Lanka and the United States.

Sri Lankan herpetologists Anslem de Silva and Ruchira Somaweera dug up a set of three illustrations published on 21 January 1888 in a newspaper in London, *The Graphic*. The first shows a European hunter measuring the spoor of a crocodile to estimate its size. The second illustrates the man negotiating with a native family for a baby. In the third, he shoots a croc that approached the tethered baby.

From 1888 to 1890, many American newspapers quoted a wanted ad from the *Ceylon Catholic Messenger*. It said 'Wanted fat babies for crocodile bait' and promised the toddlers would be returned alive. The article accompanying the ad went on to say, 'when a dark brown infant with curling toes sits on a bank and blinks at them, they [the crocodiles] throw off their cloak of laziness and make their preparations for a delicate morsel of Ceylonese humanity.'

In the early 1900s, a sailor bragged about killing four crocodiles by using babies as bait in Ceylon, and these babies were available for as little as $2 a week.

Slaves who escaped South from plantations had to brave the alligator swamps of Florida. In the late 19th and early 20th century, white folks in America used a racial slur: 'gator bait'. This gave rise to a whole industry of picture postcards, posters, and souvenirs in Florida. Images depicted open-mouthed crocodiles pasted close to a black baby while figurines were more graphic. Florida wasn't the only state to cash in on this cultural meme. A popular American song in 1899 was *Mammy's Little Alligator Bait*.

One bath soap manufacturer, unimaginatively called 'Stainilgo', featured a black infant crawling away from a crocodile. Its catch phrase: 'For the removal of discolorations'.

At least three movies were made on the subject: *Alligator Bait*, *The Gator and the Pickaninny*, and *Untamed Fury*.

On 28 January 1900, the *Washington Times* published an article: 'Phenomenal success of a photograph styled "Alligator Bait"'. It describes the popularity of a photograph of an African-American baby being used to lure alligators and reported that 'sales from this one negative have reached nearly $5,000.'

Reporter T.W. Villiers described how to procure a baby for $2 in an article *'Pickaninny bait lures voracious 'gator to death'* for a 1923 issue of the *Oakland Tribune*. The original appears to be unavailable. That same year, *Time* wrote 'coloured babies were being used for alligator bait' in Chipley, Florida. But the town's Chamber of Commerce denied it ever happened.

However, it is not clear if these accounts are true because other reports contradict them. When American newspapers such as the *Omaha Daily Bee* reproduced the article about the wanted ad from Ceylon in the 1890s, they added that American mothers would object to such a manner of dispatching crocodiles.

The British army officer, who carried a feeding bottle in his kit, wrote he had no luck finding a baby in Florida. In his hunt for alligators, he was forced to use a dog as bait. Although he was successful, he wrote, 'the sport was a good deal tamer than it would have been if I had only a baby for bait.'

Some suggest African-American mothers didn't volunteer their toddlers for this horrendous exercise. The babies were stolen from them. Unlike India and Sri Lanka, American hunters apparently didn't shoot alligators until the reptiles had swallowed the babies.

The earliest reference to the use of children to lure alligators dates from 1878. On a visit to Lee County, southwest Florida, an anonymous fisherman heard 'large hooks baited with pickaninnies' were used to lure alligators. Contrary to the claims of returning babies to their mothers unharmed, this is by far the most sickening report on the subject.

In 1919, *Richmond Times-Dispatch* announced in a tongue-in-cheek manner that authorities in Florida planned to ban the use of children 'to check the rapid disappearance of the alligator through indigestion'.

Did white hunters take the racial slur a step further and actually put it into practice? Opinion is divided. Critics argue there is no evidence of an actual event. However, many take these reports at face value.

With so many cultural references and numerous reports, and the abominable treatment of slaves, there's a possibility that babies were actually used to lure alligators. The website of the Jim Crow Museum, Michigan, says, 'It isn't really a question of whether African American babies were used as alligator bait, but the question is how frequent was the practice?'

A 1908-issue of the *Washington Times* wrote of a keeper at the New York Zoological Garden sending two African-American children into the reptile enclosure to rouse the creatures out of their winter quarters. The kids were chased by alligators much to the entertainment of the viewing public. The report pins the location and the keeper, lending it some credibility.

Although these reports overwhelmingly focus on coloured babies, hunters appear to have used white ones, too. In 1899, a report in the Kansas-based *Topeka State Journal* claimed that babies rented for 'half a dollar' from 'cracker' mothers were commonly used to lure alligators in Florida, US. 'Cracker' is a derogatory word for poor rural whites.

On 29 May 1891, the *Toronto Daily Mail* published an account from a different part of the world. An English traveller in Tsarist Russia wrote of the abominable persecution of Jews in that country. 'For a year or so hundreds of babes have been stolen and shipped to various ports on the Nile to be used as bait by the crocodile hunters. [...] The little babes serve as a bait to bring the animals on the banks, and by this means it is possible to get many animals that could not be reached in any other way.' Why didn't the kidnapping of hundreds of babies make the news? The writer said newspapers were censored and could only print news approved by the government.

How common was this horrific practice among crocodile hunters in India?

In 1894, the same year the British officer's report from India appeared in the American press, *The Evening Dispatch* of Utah published another letter from a British hunter. This man claimed the best way to kill crocs was to hook a bird or small animal and let the reptile swallow hook and bait. No mention of babies.

On 21 January 1904, Oliver Bartlett wrote of his experiences hunting a man-eating crocodile in Bargar, Orissa. In the South Carolina-based *The Bamberg Herald,* he wrote he used a puppy as bait, not a baby. He shot the crocodile but only injured it. The enraged beast knocked him down by whipping with its tail. So powerful was the blow that the man thought he might have suffered a fracture. Eventually, he killed it with another shot.

In reality, a croc would have to reach monstrous proportions to fell a man with its tail alone. Newsrooms of that time had no fact-checkers and a lot of bunkum found its way to print.

Interestingly, no hunter claimed to have used this technique in Southeast Asia. There, more prosaic baits were in vogue: a hook buried in a rotten carcass was attached to a log buoy.

A keyword search in the archives of Library of Congress throws up numerous records. But they are all of the same feeding bottle-carrying officer's letter, reproduced in other American newspapers over the following months, such as the *Record-Union*, on 1 September 1894.

Books by renowned hunters, such as *Two Years in the Jungle* by William Hornaday, published in 1885, make no mention of the use of human babies. Hornaday went hunting in the Yamuna, Chambal, Bengal, and Sri Lanka. He reports using dogs, chicken, livestock, and rotting carcasses as crocodile bait. According to a one-page profile of the man, he claimed to have used stingrays to bait the reptiles in Southeast Asia. Neither does G.P. Sanderson refer to the tactic in *Thirteen Years among the Wild Beasts of India*, published in 1878.

Mahesh Rangarajan, an environmental historian, who has extensively researched the forestry policies and hunting in British India, has not come across any reference to this practice.

The 1894 report claimed baiting with babies was a common sport, but it is the only record from India that mentions this horrendous practice. It mentions neither the name of the feeding bottle-carrying British hunter nor the area where he claims to have shot crocodiles using his favourite bait. Similarly, reports from Sri Lanka say with certainty that toddlers were the best bait and every hunter used them. The authors are anonymous and the localities where they hunted in this manner, a mystery.

A lot of sensationalist nonsense was published in the pages of newspapers of that time. Hunters tended to brag of their exploits, especially with those who didn't know any better.

Unless there is more credible evidence, the sole Indian report of this ghastly practice has to be taken with a ladle of salt.

The Night

The he real problem with kraits is that they enter homes in the dead of night and bite people in their sleep.

Kraits find their way in through gaps in the door or walls, especially during the monsoon months. They crawl along, hugging the walls or any object. A sleeping human on the floor will do. As they inch forward, they sink their hollow fangs into a finger, arm, toe, or leg. The neck, buttocks, breasts, genitals, and earlobes are not exempt.

Why do they bite with little provocation? Experts propose many theories. Sleeping people flinch when they feel the snake crawling next to them. They roll over and the animal reacts in self-defence. Humans attract kraits because they smell like prey. Body heat attracts the cold-blooded snakes. They are so hungry, they mistake parts of the human anatomy for food. Rom thinks kraits are guided by smell, and something about human body odour triggers a feeding response.

The krait's bite is almost painless and causes little or no

swelling. Often, there's not even a bite mark. Should the victim or the family switch on the light, they may not find the culprit. Kraits recoil violently from light.

Sleepy victims brush the bite off as an ant bite or the jab of a thorn. Even if they take it seriously, others may dismiss them. They'll say, 'Let's see in the morning.'

By morning, the victim lies paralysed.

* * *

Masi and Vadivelu, followed by Rom, hurried along the *bunds* that separated the fields, towards a distant knoll. I trotted to keep up. We didn't look twice at any rodent burrow on our path because we weren't after cobras. It was kraits we were after.

By some accounts, the common Indian krait is the most toxic land snake in Asia, and second only to Australia's inland taipan, in the world. Of course, every test shuffles the deck to throw up a different ranking. Whatever the test, the toxicity of krait venom ranks high, and its ability to kill is not in doubt.

As members of the Irula Snake Catchers' Cooperative, Masi and Vadivelu have a licence to catch two kraits each within the next fortnight. The cooperative buys snakes from them to extract venom to manufacture antivenom, the only antidote for a lethal snakebite.

Of the four venomous, nocturnal, rodent-eating snakes that the tribal Irulas hunt—the spectacled cobra, Russell's viper, saw-scaled viper, and common Indian krait—the last is the most difficult to find. The Irulas spend more hours on a krait hunt than on any other species. We were searching for a creature of pitch darkness that hides in the deepest burrows and emerges only late at night. I knew we were in for a long, tiring day.

Before setting out, Masi said they'd target piles of gravel dug from wells as kraits like them. They are not so common in field embankments. 'I have a hunch they are very shy snakes that don't like to be disturbed,' Rom explained. 'People walk on *bunds*, repair them. They are constantly messing with them. Nobody meddles with well tailings.'

The Irulas ambled around the gravel mound, pushing creepers out of the way with their three-foot-long iron crowbars. Several minutes later, one of the Irula men called Rom in a low voice. They pointed to a hole about an inch in diameter. It was impossibly small for a snake that grew to a metre-and-a-half long.

'How do you know the krait is in this one?' I asked in Tamil.

'Kraits push themselves through narrow holes,' Masi replied. 'When a krait goes in, it pushes soil out, so there's an even raised edge all around. See, the track is smooth not only on the lower lip, but on all sides?'

I saw a raised edge, nothing conspicuous. No matter how much I examined the hole, I didn't see the smooth tracks in the loose gravel. I slowly nodded my head, unwilling to admit I couldn't see what they so obviously did.

As soon as I stepped back, the men started digging. Was it just me? 'Can you tell if a snake has gone in?' I asked Rom quietly.

'When they point it out, I can see it,' Rom replied. 'I've never been able to spot one by myself. You need to see hundreds of thousands of burrows with krait tracks before you notice these signs.'

Since Irula kids tag along with their parents on snake hunts, they learn to pick out these subtle tracks. Rom spent forty years hunting with the tribesmen, and he still felt he lacked the training of Irula children.

* * *

Irul means 'dark' in Tamil, but it doesn't refer to their working hours, or the nocturnal snakes they hunt. The Irulas need light to pick up the subtle signs of snake activity, so they hunt during daylight hours. 'Irul' refers to their aboriginal complexion, a name given to them by skin-colour obsessed Tamilians. The Irulas call themselves *Villiyans*, or 'people with bows [and arrows]'; weapons, the Irula elders say, the British took away. How they developed their sophisticated snake tracking and natural history skills is a mystery.

The heap of gravel wasn't compacted, and the crowbars dug in with ease. The men pushed the dirt out of the way before it collapsed. Within minutes, beads of sweat became streams, running down their brows and soaking their shirts.

When on a hunt, Irula tribesmen walk all day and cannot carry many things. No tongs or hooks for these professional snake hunters; their only tool is the crowbar. When used with brute force, it becomes an earth excavator. It's a lathe when they chisel the sides of a burrow to widen it. It's a torch when the men angle the polished blade end to reflect sunlight into the dark recesses of a hole. It's a snake scooper if they find a krait or cobra—they lift the animal by supporting its belly with the crowbar in one hand and holding the tail with the other. It's a restraint used to pin a viper's head.

Now and then, Masi and Vadivelu inserted a foot-long pliant green stem they had stripped of its leaves into the hole. If it twitched on touching the coils of a snake, they knew they were close. If it hit the end of the burrow and didn't jerk, they knew the snake was no longer at home or the burrow has taken a turn. They'd look inside for more faint tracks before deciding whether to keep digging or give up.

When the twig moved, Rom and I were on our feet. The men carved the inside of the burrow, peered inside, and carefully pulled out a krait.

* * *

The metre-long snake was glossy black with an oily sheen and thin white bands. It hissed faintly. It didn't hood. It can't. Nor did it have warning colours like coral snakes. It didn't bunch up its coils, poised for a strike, like pit vipers. No krait in real life warns as Karait does in Rudyard Kipling's *Rikki Tikki Tavi*: 'Be careful. I am death!'

The animal Masi held pretended to be innocuous, like one of the many similarly banded wolf snakes. Experts will say harmless wolf snakes mimic the dangerous krait, so predators will leave them alone. If so, that trick has spectacularly backfired. People misidentify the more visible and common wolf snakes as kraits and clobber them. But it is possible kraits mimic wolf snakes to slither under the radar. More than a few escape a gruesome death as humans dither with a stick raised in mid-air. 'Maybe it's just a wolf snake.'

Twenty years ago, Rom taught me to differentiate between the identical snake species. Kraits have thin bands, he said, regularly spaced from the fore-body down to the tail. I took him at his word until we found a young 40-centimetre-long snake with wide white bands that began close behind the nape. In Parambikulam Wildlife Sanctuary in Kerala, Naseer, a friend of ours, had picked it up from under a rock and was about to gently place it in my outstretched hands. Both of us thought it was a wolf snake.

'Put it down on the ground,' Rom instructed calmly.

When Naseer put it down, Rom said, 'I think it's a krait.' Before either of us could protest, he pointed to the snake's back. 'See the line of hexagonal scales down the spine?' No mistake, it was a krait.

We had been gentle with the snake and it wasn't alarmed. It sat still, masquerading as a wolf snake, not realising its cover had been blown.

Kraits, it appears, are masters of deception. Not only do they mimic harmless wolf snakes, but they also don't stick to a template. How to instruct people to identify kraits when there are variations: in the width of bands; whether the bands are absent, paired, or not; where those ought to be; and even if the colour of the snake ranges from brown to black?

When Masi let the snake go, it covered its head with its coils and pretended we weren't there. Instead of trying to make a quick getaway, all it wanted to do was hide. The most dangerous snake in India is a scaredy-cat when the sun is up. But at night, the krait transforms into Mr Hyde.

'They won't bite unprovoked,' Rom has always maintained of snakes. 'Only in self-defence. To avoid getting bitten, use a torch at night and wear footwear.' Most bites by cobras and vipers occur when rural people trample on them in the dark, after they finish work in their fields or dash to the neighbour's when the sugar runs out.

But the krait: that's another animal entirely.

* * *

Krait venom is packed with powerful neurotoxins. The first symptom of the venom's action is drooping eyelids. Sometimes, victims complain of severe abdominal pain that forces them to seek help. The extremities tingle as the venom shuts down nerves and progressively paralyses the body. When the muscles can't pump the diaphragm anymore, the victim develops difficulty in breathing and swallowing. Within minutes, he or she can no longer move.

The Rajasthanis say *peona*, or krait, sits on the chest of a sleeping person and sucks their breath. It is an accurate, if metaphorical, description of respiratory failure caused by krait bite.

Toxins bind themselves to nerves and are impervious to antivenom. Injecting antivenom neutralizes free-floating toxins in blood and tissues only. More than antivenom, totally paralyzed patients need ventilators to keep them going. Or they become deprived of oxygen and die.

We've heard of families assuming the seemingly lifeless victims were dead. They didn't seek immediate medical attention. The victims died, but much later.

What makes krait bite a horror story is that although a victim appears lifeless, he or she is fully conscious. Of all the things that go 'bump' in the night, this is the worst. What must go through the mind of a person who's unable to communicate and is locked in a body over which he or she has no control?

Rom worked for Bill Haast of the Miami Serpentarium for two years in his youth. Haast survived almost 200 bites by venomous snakes, including king cobras and mambas, over his fifty-six-year career. Of all those bites, only one nearly killed him, and that was by a common Indian krait. He maintained a journal of his developing symptoms as long as he was able.

'Every muscle in my body aches,' he wrote five hours after the bite. 'Pins and needles sensation on soles of feet. Throat very sore, teeth hurt, back of tongue is numb. My speech and thought processes do not seem to be affected.'

Several minutes later: 'Radio and other sounds are tremendously magnified. Colours of the curtains seem more brilliant.' He told Rom a few years later that the sound of a cough sounded like an explosion.

'I felt like the skin had been stripped from my body,' Haast told the Associated Press in 1996. '... like every nerve in my teeth was exposed, like my hair was being ripped out of my head.'

He had an out-of-body experience, floating above the room and looking down at the doctors and nurses working to save his life. Although he wasn't religious, he said he saw the white face of a lamb. He heard one doctor say, 'He's fading, he's fading.' Although helpless, he willed the medical team to keep working.

* * *

What should people do to avoid getting bitten by kraits?

Obviously, sleeping off the ground was the answer, or so I believed for a long time. Sleeping on the first floor was even better. However, one study in Nepal found that almost 70 per cent of the victims were asleep on a cot, and more than 70 per cent were on the first floor. That's surprising, because kraits seem reluctant to climb. But in Nepali study, they seemed to target people who were out of reach, rather than those sleeping on the floor. The only thing that prevented krait bites was sleeping under mosquito nets.

If they climb up the legs of beds and haul themselves up the stairs, then Rom may be right. Human body odour seems to attract kraits like bees to nectar.

They are also adept escape artists. Kraits put their ability to jam themselves into the littlest burrows to use when imprisoned in a bag. They thrust their noses against the cloth tirelessly. If it gives, they shove themselves through.

Freshly caught snakes bite and smear their venom on the cloth snake bags. Venom corrodes the fabric over time. So Rom held up the snake bag our krait was going into against the light, pulling the cloth apart to test for weaknesses.

When he was sure the bag was good, he held it out and Masi dropped the krait into it. He twisted the open end and tied it into a tight knot. The men put on their shirts and we continued the hunt for more kraits.

Until recently, Masi and Vadivelu lived in thatched mud huts. They would have observed kraits entering their homes through gaps in rickety doors. Perhaps they knew more about krait behaviour.

'Why do you think kraits bite people?' I asked Vadivelu.

'It's the person's fate; their time has come.'

A Monsoon Spectacle

Life in Agumbe, hills of Karnataka, is defined by rains. Residents count down or up to it. Visitors' jaws drop when they hear the place soaks up to 10 metres of rain annually. But all that precipitation doesn't fall gently or evenly across the year. Most of it comes in one concentrated downpour over four months, from June to September. Agumbe sits at the top and the very edge of an escarpment, smack in the way of monsoon clouds sweeping inland from the Arabian Sea. The topography traps the clouds until they've spent their force.

I didn't know any of this when I first visited the place more than twenty years ago. Agumbe was the centre of Rom's universe since he had caught a pair of king cobras single-handedly in the early 1970s.

Within months of becoming an item, Rom and I went camping in Agumbe. I grew up in the city; I had not seen a forest; and I knew nothing about wildlife. I imagined the Agumbe forest would look like the pictures in the National

Geographic magazine: vividly-coloured macaws flying across the greenery; cute chimpanzees gambolling around; and orange orangutans hanging off tree branches. If I had investigated a little, I would have realized we were going to the wettest place in South India. I was so ill-prepared for the trip and I didn't know it.

Trees of the Agumbe forest were stately high-rises. Dreadlocks of moss trailed from branches. The thick wet leaf litter muffled our footfalls. The forest smelt dank and mouldy.

To an outsider, I must have seemed like a demure bride, following her husband with her head bent down. I was hypnotized by the ground that was seething with brown worms. Unlike plump white maggots, these brown ones were lean and mean. The lot of them were making their way to us. Like a heroic zombie-slayer, Rom breezily dismissed them, 'Ha, leeches.' More than their dietary preference for warm blood, I was terrified of contact—of their cold, slimy bodies attached to mine. The very thought made me feel icky.

The monotonous strumming of cicadas reached a deafening crescendo, and when the insects couldn't twang at a higher pitch, they fell silent only to try again. The steady drone gave me a headache.

I didn't realize one had to walk so much. Sweat dripped from the tip of my nose. I was too tired to wipe it away and it ran into my mouth. I expected wild animals to stroll past, fly over, and swing from branch to branch, but we had seen nothing for several hours. Some little birds called from the canopy, but they weren't flashy like toucans. When I mentioned this, Rom said toucans weren't found in this continent. Nor were sloths and scarlet macaws. Or orangutans. I felt short-changed; those glossy pictures in magazines had made forests look glamorous.

Rom strode through the forest, looking under logs, peering into tree hollows, and sticking twigs into burrows. Apparently, you have to work hard to find anything that moves. I dragged my feet behind him, trying hard to lighten up. If only I could focus, I'd be fine, I thought as I mimicked him. He hopped like a goat from rock to rock to cross the stream. It seemed easy but I didn't have his sense of balance. I slipped and fell, and now I was cold and wet. I began to hate the forest and longed to return home.

None of our subsequent forest trips over the years fazed me. I learned about elephants, nettles, hornbills, and snakes. I adopted Rom's disdain when anyone else complained of leeches. Agumbe had become my touchstone for jungle camping.

However, when Rom talked of setting up a research station there, the mere thought of returning gave me the heebie-jeebies.

A decade after my first visit, Rom and I returned to Agumbe, in 2004. By then, I wanted to confront my demons. Was it as bad as I remembered?

As soon as we entered the forest, I looked for familiar elements. Long streamers of moss gave the forest a timeless fairy tale allure. Massive buttresses that helped top-heavy trees stand upright looked like the fins of a rocket. This time, I took a deep breath and recognized the earthy fragrance of humus. The path was sprinkled with orange flowers and jade green fruits. The forest was the same, but I had changed. I couldn't believe I had been such a wimp. We drove deeper and deeper into the jungle but couldn't find our old campsite. The jungle had probably reclaimed it.

We followed another track that led to a farmstead in the midst of the forest. Behind an old-fashioned house, coffee and cardamom grew in the shade of areca palms. The house overlooked terraced rice fields that extended down to a stream. We met the family, and Rom enquired if they would consider selling their charming spread. The head of the family replied, indeed, they would.

We asked if they saw any king cobras. The old man shook his head vehemently.

Leopards?

No.

Wild dogs?

No.

Any snakes?

No.

Do you see any animals here at all?

No, never.

He had mistaken us for lily-livered city people.

Rom's mother gave him money to buy the land, and the Whitley Fund for Nature gave an award to build a research station.

Agumbe was a wonderful place in fair weather. Giant squirrels kept up a constant chatter, racket-tailed drongoes baffled us with their mimicry, and shy langurs spied on us. Word percolated out to neighbouring villages that Rom and his assistant caught king cobras. Villagers frequently called in the dry pre-monsoon months for help in moving the world's largest venomous snakes. This was the king cobra mating season, and lust-driven snakes blundered into homes, in their hunt for mates. They took refuge in roofs, bathrooms, barns, and kitchens. We hadn't heard of any other place in India with so many king cobras.

That first year in Agumbe was a lesson in monsoon-living. Just before the rains arrived, the village bustled with activity. The terracotta-tiled roofs had to be fixed so they didn't leak. If they did, nothing could be done until the rains stopped. So nobody took a chance.

Following the villagers' lead, we nailed clear plastic sheets to windows and draped long strips of blue tarpaulin around the granite posts of the verandah, completely enveloping the house.

As we went back and forth ferrying supplies, we ran into groups of women returning from the forest with baskets of mushrooms and bushels of leaf litter. Through the monsoon months, villagers line the floor of their cattle sheds with dry leaves. When the substrate got soiled with urine and dung, women removed the whole lot to compost and spread a fresh layer of leaves. Without the lining, the floor would need washing, and in the monsoon, it would never dry.

During these expeditions, women found king cobra nests. Female snakes heavy with eggs gather dry leaves lying on the forest floor into a mound, a feat performed by no other snake in the world. These nests have to withstand the monsoonal battering and keep the eggs inside dry. Pregnant king cobras repeatedly crawl repeatedly to compress the fluffy pile of leaves. As the leaves get compacted, they add another layer of leaves and pack it down. When they have a foot-high stack, they slither into it and lay their eggs. Once done, they pile more leaves on top and tamp down. A finished nest stands about a metre tall and a metre in diameter, a tempting sight for anyone looking to quickly fill their basket with leaves. Often, the mother king cobra stays with her nest for a few weeks, giving the women the fright of their lives.

The anticipation of the rains ran high in the last week of May, as everyone hurried through their chores. Mornings scorched, while thunderstorms cooled the afternoons. In kitchens, women were busy pickling vegetables in salt and stocking up on rotund Madras cucumbers. They hung these gourds from the rafters, where they'd last for months. Once the rains began, there would be no fresh vegetables except green leafy vegetables and the cucumbers. These days, however, vegetables are trucked in from the plains and there's a greater variety of fresh produce.

The monsoon sets in gently, with no fanfare. And people don't welcome it with festivals. Despite the precautions, it was a battle to keep moisture out. The terracotta roof tiles absorbed so much water, the inside was always wet. Heat from the wood fire in the kitchen did little to dry the roof. Moisture condensed on the walls and settled on beds, clothes, and books. Everything felt not just damp, but wet to the touch.

One morning, we came upon Rom's assistant standing in the kitchen with a towel wrapped around his waist, toasting his underwear over the stove. We knew then we had to build better residences for researchers if they were to stay and work comfortably. The key was double-roofing. The roof is the most expensive part of building construction; to have two almost doubled the budget. But the innovation was worth it, and the new residences were drier than the farmhouse.

Rom initiated a research project in collaboration with Matt Goode of the University of Arizona. They implanted radio transmitters in four king cobras to see if they had a territory. Researchers followed the snakes through sun and rain. The thick vegetation halved the radios' effective radius. If they lost a snake, we weren't sure if we'd find it again. Like tigers have territories, we learned these snakes, too, lived within the confines of their home ranges. They had favourite hiding spots to which they returned repeatedly.

In Hindu mythology, elephants are said to be dark monsoon clouds, grounded and mortal. And Indra, the rain god, rides Airavata, the white elephant, across the skies. Although no elephants had come through these forests for decades, two bulls from Chikmagalur started visiting for a few months every year. Otherwise, this is one of the few forests one can walk without fear of being chased by a pachyderm. Although Agumbe abuts Kudremukh National Park, tigers were scarce as were spotted deer. Perhaps, these animals find the forest too dense and wet. Leopards, spotted and black, wandered through the research station.

A pack of dholes lived nearby, and we were often woken at night by the desperate shrieks of sambhar being killed. In drier forests, we would fear elephants and sloth bears, but Agumbe was the realm of king cobras, frogs, and leeches.

On my first visit, I had been terrorized by the nature of the forest—the tall trees that obliterate sunlight and rainfall to end all life on the planet. Contrary to fairy tales and mythology, these were precisely the conditions that fostered life. The lack of large, heavyset mammals was more than compensated by the sheer diversity of other forms of life. For numerous creatures, the monsoon is the time of procreation.

Large, green female flying frogs carried small males piggyback to ponds. Perched just above the water, she started spawning. The male whipped up the spawn with his hind legs like an eggbeater, until it resembled a large dollop of meringue. The egg mass hung suspended until tadpoles emerged and dropped into the water below.

A pair of a recently discovered frog species mated while doing a handstand. Then the female laid her eggs on a twig overhanging water, while standing on her hands. After she was done, the male picked up globs of mud and patted them around the eggs. Did the mud pack protect the spawn from predators? Experts don't know yet. But as far as they know, no other frog in the world behaves in this charming manner.

King cobra nests may be little more than piles of leaves, but they weather the battering by the rains better than you'd expect. Water runs off the surface of the tightly packed mounds. Humidity in the interior of the nest is not high enough for fungus to grow and not low enough for the soft, leathery eggs to dry out. That's far better than we managed with our double-roofed houses.

We kept cameras inside three layers of Ziplock bags. Laptops snuggled in waterproof Pelican cases. Despite the elaborate care, fungus etched pretty designs inside camera lenses. Computers displayed unintelligible error messages or crashed. Dehumidifiers needed electricity, and we had meagre solar power. Our attempts to tap one of the seasonal streams with a micro hydel power generator failed. Those king cobra nests may look primitive, but they serve their purpose well.

Through the monsoon, while the embryos continued to grow, we anticipated the adults would hunker down in burrows and wait out the rains. Instead, one male king cobra implanted with a radio transmitter went snacking. In sixteen weeks, he ate twenty-six pit vipers. These 50-gram snakes were like peanuts for the 5-kilogram giant. He hunted them down by scent, climbing up trees, bushes, vines, and across the forest floor in heavy rain. The amount of effort he put into getting each little snake seemed disproportionate.

One hapless pregnant pit viper, on whose trail the king cobra had latched, tried to make a break for it. She plunged into a pond and swam to the other bank, where she lay still. The brown splotches on the back camouflaged her. Dogs lose scent trails when their quarries enter the water. So we expected the king cobra to come to the water's edge and give up in frustration.

We watched in horror as the king cobra flicked his tongue on the water surface and inexorably tracked down the pit viper. There was no escape for the little snake. We were thankful to be humans and not pit vipers.

With snakes on the move, trackers couldn't take time off. Dhiraj, one of the young trackers, was following a king cobra when it turned around and approached him. He froze and waited for it to move along. The snake unhurriedly flicked its tongue on the ground, perhaps picking up some interesting odour. While he stood still as a statue, a leech inched its way up his neck and on his face. Dhiraj didn't want to disturb the snake, so he didn't move. When the leech came to his mouth, he chewed it to death and spat it out. That's the only meat to pass Dhiraj's lips.

Monsoon is also a season of activity for villagers. Farmers ploughed their slushy fields and tended areca palms. While raincoats and umbrellas were common, farm workers still used the *kurumbu*, a broad, stiff cape made of dry *dhoop* (White dammar) leaves. The hood hooks over the head, covering the shoulders and back, perfect for working hunched over in rice fields. Many residents' feet were stained purple with tincture of iodine to prevent foot rot. Kasturiakka, the lady of the largest house in the village, served *kashayam*, a hot, fragrant brew of nineteen spices that wards off cold, to visitors.

After days of not seeing the sun, I asked her one day, 'Do you ever feel you've had enough rain? Do you pray to Indra to turn it off?'

'Yes we do,' she replied.

The rain temple, 35 kilometres away in Kigga, was not dedicated to Indra, as I had expected, but to the antler-headed Rishya Shringeswara, a young, celibate sage. The story goes that he summoned the rain god when the country of Angada was hit by famine. Although I couldn't find a story of Shringeswara sending rain clouds away, devotees also pray to him to limit rainfall. But how much was too much? For villagers used to a deluge every year, what would warrant a trip to Kigga? I haven't found an answer.

I asked Kasturiakka the meaning of Agumbe. I assumed the exotic, almost African sounding name meant something like 'the place where rain clouds dump their goods'.

'Agumbe is short for Madagumbapura,' she replied. 'It means "the place with lots of elephants."'

The fluid that leaks from the temples of male elephants in *musth*, a period of testosterone-driven aggression, is called 'mada', according to mythologist Devdutt Pattnaik.

Agumbe is an ironic name for a forest with hardly any elephants. But Kasturiakka said it wasn't named for wild elephants, but the many captive elephants that aided logging operations a long time ago. Perhaps, a more appropriate meaning is, 'the playing fields of celestial elephants in musth.'

I may not have wrangled giant, dangerous snakes, but Agumbe marked my own rite of passage. Indra's celestial elephants sent me running once, but now I'm drawn to see the annual monsoonal spectacle they unleash on the land.

Acknowledgments

This collection of stories exists because of many people. Mukund Padmanabhan commissioned the column *My Husband and Other Animals* in the English daily *The Hindu*. It was G. Ananthakrishnan's idea to pitch the column to Mukunth. More than the previous selection, readers moulded this compendium by asking questions. In some cases, my answers took the shape of full-length articles.

By far the most challenging article to write was *Why do Men Rape?* Not only did I rely on papers on biology but I drew extensively from the writings of feminist philosopher Griet Vandermassen, anthropologist Melissa Emery Thompson, and women's studies scholar Barbara Watson.

Many long-suffering friends answered my incessant questions – Rauf Ali, Vidya Athreya, Aniruddha Belsare, Jack Frazier, Priyadarshini Govind, Manori Gunawardena, Pradip Krishen, Shyamal Lakshminarayanan, M.D. Madhusudhan, Divya Mudappa, Mahesh Rangarajan,

Pavithra Sankaran, Kartik Shanker, Rick Shine, Anindya Sinha, Harold Voris, David Warrell, and David Williams.

Our families – Gail and John Wynne, Neel and Arundhati Chattopadhyaya, Nina and Ram Menon, and Anand Pillai and Nivedita Sahasrabudhe – encouraged my writing. Rom was subject, inspiration, and foil for many tales, and my parents, K.R. Lenin and Sivakami, were indefatigable readers of every story.

Firstpost published Did Crocodile Hunters use Babies as Bait in India?, Scroll published an edited version of Snake Oil Merchants, and The Indian Quarterly published The Night and A Monsoon Spectacle.

I thank them all.